STUDIES IN STRUCTURAL SOCIOLOGY

Other Notable Gordian Knot Books

Putting Universal Human Rights to Work: Policy Actions in the Struggle for Social Justice, by Archibald Stuart, PhD

Malthus, Darwin, Durkheim, Marx, Weber, Ibn Khaldûn: On Human Species Survival, by Walter L. Wallace, PhD

Seminal Sociological Writings: From Auguste Comte to Max Weber: An Anthology of Groundbreaking Works that Created the Science of Sociology, edited by Richard Altschuler, PhD

Seminal Sociological Writings, Vol. 2: From Harriet Martineau to W. E. B. Du Bois: An Anthology of Groundbreaking Works that Created the Science of Sociology, edited by Richard Altschuler, PhD

On the Cutting Edge: Tales of a Cold War Engineer at the Dawn of the Nuclear, Guided Missile, Computer, and Space Ages, by Robert Brodsky, PhD

Women, Marriage, and Wealth, by Joyce A. Joyce, PhD

Where Are We Going? by Miriam Finder Tasini, MD

Reflections on Medicine: Essays by Robert U. Massey, MD, edited by Martin Duke, MD

Contemplative Aging: A Way of Being in Later Life, by Edmund Sherman, PhD

Law and Society, by Stanford M. Lyman, PhD

On Being a Woman Surgeon: Sixty Women Share Their Stories, edited by Preeti R. John, MD

Doctor, Why Does My Face Still Ache? Getting Relief from Persistent Jaw, Ear, and Headache Pain, by Donald R. Tanenbaum, DDS, and S. L. Roistacher, DDS

Dancing on the Tails of the Bell Curve: Readings on the Joy and Power of Statistics, edited by Richard Altschuler, PhD

Identifying and Recovering from Psychological Trauma: A Psychiatrist's Guide for Victims of Childhood Abuse, Spousal Battery, and Political Terrorism, by Brian Trappler, MD

The Gay & Lesbian Marriage & Family Reader: Analyses of Problems and Prospects for the 21st Century, edited by Jennifer M. Lehmann, PhD

STUDIES IN STRUCTURAL SOCIOLOGY

by

Frank W. Young

Gordian Knot Books
An Imprint of Richard Altschuler & Associates, Inc.

Los Angeles

Studies in Structural Sociology. Copyright © 2015 by Frank W. Young. For information contact the publisher, Gordian Knot Books, at 10390 Wilshire Boulevard, Los Angeles, CA 90024, (424) 279-9118, or send an email to Richard.Altschuler@gmail.com.

Library of Congress Control Number: 2014957790
CIP data for this book are available from the Library of Congress

ISBN-13: 978-1-884092-70-1

Gordian Knot Books is an imprint of
Richard Altschuler & Associates, Inc.

Cover Design: Josh Garfield

Printed in the United States of America

Distributed by Ingram

To Lorrie

CONTENTS

INTRODUCTION

This collection of essays and research articles introduces a new socio-logical paradigm—"structural ecology"—that is structural and causal. It parts company with economic and other sectoral disciplines by sub-stituting appropriate indicators of population health for measures of economic or political success, and by taking the whole community as its unit of analysis. Individuals are treated as a special case of community. Communities, large and small, are conceptualized as adapting to a chang-ing physical and social environment by constant social problem-solving. The explanation of how communities adapt and improve their population health turns on the ratio of problem-solving capacity to serious threats, such as the loss of a major resource, displacement by another ethnic group, or an epidemic with no known cure. Problem-solving capacity, in turn, is defined as combinations of the three most frequent problem-solving strategies: the application of specialized knowledge, debating alternatives, and mobilizing behind reforms.

Structural theory defines communities as multi-functional groups with a concern for their members. This definition spans groups as small as the household and as large as the nation-state. The sum total of these communities comprises most of the social organization on the planet, because all the other forms—such as bureaucracies, networks, or in-stitutions—are considered parts of communities. The many levels of community are important in this theory because population health must be measured comparatively within levels. The communities themselves must be measured systemically and with level-specific indicators. Changes in institutions are recognized but their contribution to the deter-mination of population health is minimal.

Structural ecology is a version of the Chicago social ecological tradition with a number of differences, which will emerge in the four sec-tions of this book. It is also neo-Darwinian and neo-Durkheimian. It re-flects the Darwinian tradition in focusing on the causation of population health levels as a consequence of the interaction of problem-solving capacity (instead of mutations) and threats, instead of random environ-mental changes. It reflects the Durkheimian tradition in focusing on whole communities and the variations in population health at each level, from households to the nation-state. It therefore rejects the "individual in society" interpretation of Durkheim that is still dominant in some parts of sociology.

The articles in this book illustrate these themes. Starting with anthropology, the other three categories become more theoretical and "positive" in the sense of explaining sociological phenomena directly, instead of by way of rejecting explanations that already exist in the literature. The introductions to the four categories refer to specific features of articles within the three broad themes of this paradigm: non-economic, structural and causal.

As is evident, the articles in this book are arranged in approximate chronological order, from 1967 to 2012. They end, in the fourth section, with a comprehensive theoretical statement followed by illustrations of the theory's applicability. This order will be intrinsically interesting for some readers because it reflects the development of the paradigm. But the last four articles make a larger point which is that in the changing globalized world, the frequency of communities large and small that are "left behind" has increased, spawning many nativistic movements, some of which have reached new levels of violence and brutality. Accordingly, some readers may wish to begin with the articles in the last section and their potential for making sense out of a currently turbulent world.

SECTION 1
ANTHROPOLOGY

Overview

The article on incest taboos initiates this section because it is a classic problem as yet unsettled, and it reflects many stylistic features in social research that have become more prominent in the last several decades. The first of these is the need for abstract concepts measured by the particular empirical indicators, as in the solidarity-incest taboo relationship. A related point is the need to explain deviant cases. A third feature is the application of statistics when samples are available. My strong advocacy of these and similar characteristics marked me early on as a "sociologist." In retrospect, it is perhaps not surprising that this article has never been cited by anthropologists, even in their comprehensive bibliographies. Such was and still is the antipathy between the two disciplines.

The study of folktales has always been important in anthropology, because it is widely believed that folktales reflect important features of the communities that sustain them. This comparison of three interpretations of a Plains Indians folktale continues that tradition, while warning that some of these interpretations are virtually untestable. Since this article was written, "textual analysis" has made significant progress, especially now that computer programs are capable of extracting complex patterns from texts. It is too early to claim that the social world can be construed as "wall-to-wall texts," but with the computerization of newspapers and similar sources we may be approaching something like that.

My reconceptualization of Redfield's folk-urban continuum was written more than fifty years after he published his study of Yucatán communities (in 1941). Consequently, it uses sociological concepts that are more fully developed in the last set of papers in this book on structural ecology. As such, it continues a tradition of working with older theories for the purpose of generating new ideas that is as old as science. Unfortunately, this aspect of science tends to be overshadowed by the pressure for empirical tests. They are important but so is innovation in theory, which is here illustrated by separating the two poles of the folk-urban continuum, in order to create a dimension of urbanization and another of nativism, thereby refining the original concepts of "disorgani-zation" and "folkness." Implicit in this exercise is the deeper aim of breaking with the European tradition of polar types.

The last paper in this set summarizes the present state of a technique of data collection that is as old as bureaucracies and reinvented more often than the wheel: the "informant interview." This technique is simply a standard set of questions about the institutions and organization of a sample of comparable units, such as bureaucracies, village communities, or provinces. Unlike the "key informant" technique, which is used to gather specialized information about a community that is then syn-thesized into an "ethnography" or a newspaper article, the data from in-formant interview surveys can be used in statistical analyses. In this form it ought to be a standard technique; but anthropologists have avoided it in favor of case studies, while sociologists mostly prefer household or individual questionnaires. The informant survey falls between these two stools. That awkward status will probably not change until sociology lives up to its name and concentrates on the study of groups.

INCEST TABOOS AND SOCIAL SOLIDARITY

Abstract: *Incest taboos, defined broadly as prohibitions on emotional alliances among group members, may be interpreted as one of a range of indicators of high solidarity. The "incest taboo problem," therefore, dissolves because the real object of explanation is solidarity. This article proposes a cross cultural test of this interpretation. Functional interpretations that stress the preservation of existing role relations, although superficially similar, are seen to lead to different research consequences. Case material on the emotional aversions among age mates in collective settlements in Israel and the incestuous marriages of Egyptian royalty are interpreted.*

A serial reading of the many proposed explanations of the incest taboo problem, along with the critiques of opposing theories that the authors usually supply, suggests not that one is right and the others wrong, but that they are all inadequate. In short, the critiques (Aberle 1963; Coult 1963) are better than the theories. When any research area reaches such a state, it seems reasonable to assume that the problem has not been formulated correctly.

Although it is not the purpose of this paper to review once again the available interpretations and their alleged deficiencies, it will be useful to the ensuing discussion simply to list them. As given by Aberle et al. (1963), they are: the inbreeding theory, which emphasizes the deleterious genetic consequences of not observing an incest taboo; the family theory, which states that incest taboos prohibit unregulated sexual competition that would disrupt the group; the social and cultural system theory, which stresses the advantages of the interfamilial links brought about by the operation of the incest taboo; and the demographic theory, which holds that the conditions under which early man lived made it impossible for him to do other than breed out. There are also others, such as the view that the incest taboo forces the child to be interested in social objects other than his family, and the notion that there is an instinctive horror of sexual contact with a member of one's family.

Just as the available interpretations—it is pretentious to call them theories—are now well catalogued, so are most of the main facts to be explained. In the first place, despite the widespread misuse of the word, the incest taboo is not universal. Although the evidence is vague and subject to many interpretations, it appears that incest taboos do not exist in some isolated or disorganized groups or for some royal personages. Granted the difficulty of clarifying these exceptions, it is still strange that almost no writer has attempted to use them as a supreme test of an interpretation.

The frequency of the incest taboo, which is almost universal in nuclear families, is only a component of another basic fact: its application varies from this minimum range to a wide variety of kin types. Murdock (1949) documented this wide variation in detail, and, among other points, he stressed the fact that incest taboos are never confined to the nuclear family. These facts of variation have not so much been ignored as they have been brushed aside. Thus, a professional group like that represented by the Aberle et al. report, deals in detail with the incest taboo within the nuclear family, and then blandly states: "Once the familial taboo is in existence, extensions of the taboo to other categories of kin become a simple evolutionary step."(Aberle 1963:263)

Of course, the "facts" that a theory explains are, at least in part, indicated by the theory itself. What is a fact for one may be ignored by another, although surely the foregoing list is difficult to ignore from any point of view. What is more interesting is the way some formulations call attention to previously ignored empirical patterns as legitimate challenges for the theory. In the present case, it will be suggested that the extension of the rule of endogamy, as well as exogamy, is problematical, and, in addition, that there are many instances of prohibition of emotional alliances which, from a wider view, should be considered "incest."

A Reformulation of the Incest Problem

As conventionally defined, the "incest taboo in any society consists of a set of prohibitions which outlaw heterosexual relationships between various categories of kinsmen" (Aberle et al. 1963). Thus, the problem is to explain under what conditions such a phenomenon occurs and why it persists. What is needed is simply a statement of the type "If A, then B," or more precisely, "The greater the A, the greater the B," when the latter term is taken to be the elaboration or extension of incest prohibitions.

But here lies the flaw in all available explanations of incest taboos. They do not distinguish between concept and measure. If you ask what an incest prohibition is, you are told about the kinds of statements that are made in primitive tribes, or the laws on the books of many countries, or the kinds of reactions people give to the mere possibility of sexual contact with a close relative of the opposite sex. When you ask what incest taboos are conceptually, you are likely to receive either no answer or no more than a repetition of the nominal definition. Of course, the importance of distinguishing concept and measure is not universally conceded; sufficient to say that it is the starting point of the present attempt at reformulating the problem.

It is proposed here that the conceptual referent of incest taboos is group solidarity. If this concept is defined as the degree to which the members of a group cooperate to create, maintain, and project a unified definition of their situation, it is clear that incest taboos—which may now be more widely interpreted as the prohibition of emotional alliances among persons who have been defined as ingroup members—reflect solidarity. They are concrete evidence that no subgroups exist to undermine the over-all coordination of the larger group. Although incest prohibitions are negative communications, they exist alongside many positive rituals and beliefs as ways that groups express solidarity.

It follows that incest is not simply a matter of sexual relations among relatives; that is merely the formulation for groups that use the vocabulary of kinship. In religions, there are emotional bonds among heretics or backsliders; in political parties, there are plotters or revisionists. Nepotism rules exist in bureaucracies to keep down heterosexual coalitions that may become administratively difficult; and in divorce proceedings, where the court defines a wider membership for the married couple, one speaks of prohibiting collusion. In short, "incest" is potentially all around us, and prohibitions develop wherever there is solidarity because that is part of what we mean by solidarity. In his discussion of "ideological groups"—which seem equivalent to what are here called "solidary groups"—Nahirny "(1962:398) sums up the general empirical fact: "It is one of the most striking and general features of ideological groups that they frown upon and oppose vehemently any display of personal affective attachments among their members."

An alternative way of managing a potentially disruptive emotional alliance is to define a person as a non-member. Thus, the *berdache* or transvestite role in some Plains Indian bands sets apart a man who might want to pair off with another man. In other primitive groups, menstrual taboos serve to exclude women from participating in the solidarity of men. The question arises: Why is marriage allowed? Is not a married couple an emotional alliance that undermines the solidarity of any larger group, such as an extended family, a clan, or a religious community? The solidarity interpretation clearly requires the prohibition of marriage in highly solidary groups, but the problem now shifts to that of defining the boundary of the in-group. If the nuclear family is the only viable solidary group, then the incest taboo must necessarily fall on the children. If the parents are separated, the group would cease to exist. If, however, the nuclear family is a component of a larger unit, such as a corporate kin group, the marriage bond must be weakened until such time as the couple learns the necessary reserve. Thus, young men are forced to find wives outside the unit, and then such women are permanently delineated as outsiders by means of unilineal kin terms and other such labeling. There may also be separate compounds for men and women, and senior women who can now be trusted not to disrupt things are put in charge of the younger women. Even allowing these rather affectively neutral marriages indicates that few corporate groups can maintain very high solidarity. Of course, there are cases of utopian communities or even nations that have, at the height of their revolutionary fervor, attempted to outlaw marriage.

Although solidary groups tend to have more negative prohibitions, more "repressive law," they also show many positive expressions. Concretely, one observes concerted (but not homogeneous) activity, an elaborated ideology, a clearly defined role structure, strong sanctions in all aspects of life, and sharp delineation of ingroup and outgroup membership, punctuated frequently by outgroup hostility. Citing Nahirny again: "The clearer the line of demarcation, the more intense is the hatred and suspicions of the outside world and, consequently, the more cohesive the ideological group" (1962:402). In these many ways, the group defines itself and its objectives sharply.

An alternative way to state the essential nature of the solidary group is the following hypothesis: The greater the solidarity, the more dramatic will be the customs surrounding any shift in the pattern of roles within it. Although this statement merely spins out the definition, it is useful because it highlights, by definition, a solidary group employing a particular form of communication, namely, dramatization. This is communication that combines symbols in such a way that the probability of a particular interpretation is increased. When a nation, particularly one lacking a large industrial plant, sets off an atomic bomb, it is a dramatic communication. Similarly, martyrdom and ritual suicide are classic instances of the dramatic mode.

If dramatization varies directly with solidarity, one should expect elaborate role-transition ceremonies where solidarity is high. In families and family-like systems, one's attention is drawn to ceremonies like marriage, funerals, initiations, and parenthood recognition (misnamed the *couvade*). Similarly, rites of degradation, such as public punishment or banishment, will occur. Incest taboos fall between these two types of rituals in that they deal with behavior which, if permitted, would redefine and, perhaps, undermine the role coordination required for solidarity, even if the system continued to exist. We may call them rites of "placement" or "containment." Here the list includes avoidance rules, joking relationships, rituals of embarrassment, and a variety of means by which people are "put down" or "in their place." How then do incest taboos vary in the degree of dramatization? A scale based on the kind of data found in the Human Relations Area Files is beyond the scope of this paper, but in general one notes the variation in the extent of application and the intensity of the communication.

Exogamy, the rule requiring men to find wives outside the residence unit, must surely index a high level of solidarity because its negative aspect—the incest prohibition—is typically communicated non-verbally. This interpretation suggests that the strength of rules of endogamy— those that define an outer boundary of choice of spouse—may also express solidarity. In addition to the already mentioned concern with the line between ingroup and outgroup, solidary groups strongly attempt to retain their members and to expand their membership. As an extreme, they develop techniques for changing outgroup members into ingroup members (e.g., propaganda, conversion, and, brainwashing). In primitive societies, the kinship classification system is manipulated for this purpose, but a clear outer boundary of this activity is maintained. Thus, solidarity contains a double and contradictory thrust: expand the membership but keep it pure. Applied to mate selection, the rule enjoins men in patrilocal communities to choose women outside their group who are, nonetheless, closely related. In the case of the *kibbutz*, as Talmon (1964:506) notes, young people choose spouses who come from outside their collective settlement but who are still members of the collective movement. In general, the greater the solidarity, the narrower will be the belt of acceptable spouses defined by the rules of exogamy and endogamy.

Thus, the interpretation of the concrete phenomena of incest taboos as manifestations of solidarity is possible and heuristic. But a possible obstacle is that the transformation of the dependent variable to an aspect of solidarity merely poses a new question: What determines high and low solidarity? Although the question is legitimate, it will not get a satisfactory answer here. The present claim is that reformulating the question from "what determines incest taboos?" to the causes of solidarity will move us closer to a solution because it facilitates actual empirical tests, the comparison of incest prohibitions with cognate phenomena, and because it articulates with the available theory about solidarity.

Despite the independent origins of this formulation, other interpretations, particularly those that stress the function of incest taboos for the group, are almost equivalent. The difference may appear to boil down to one of terminology, with "function" and "maintenance of boundaries" appearing in earlier formulations while "index" and "solidarity" are used here. But differences in terminology should not be underestimated; they typically reflect divergent cognitive worlds. That is, in fact, the basic claim of this paper: It is impossible to understand the phenomenon of incest taboos without thinking in the concept-operation, hypothesis-testing framework that has become a common language of sociologists since World War II.

It is certainly true that writers from Malinowski to Talmon have seen a relationship between incest taboos and group solidarity. As Malinowski (1931) put it, "by dissociating the disruptive and competitive element from workaday cooperation [exogamy] fulfills once more an important cultural function." Talmon goes on to concede that "This elucidation of functions . . . does not explain differential incidence. To account for the adoption of a certain institution it is not sufficient to show that it is in some sense 'good' for society and serves its long-range interests" (1964:498). Neither is it sufficient, one might add, to concentrate on a part of the problem when the real object of explanation is something more abstract. Considering incest taboos to be an index of something else redirects the search for a causal explanation, and in this case it directs attention to the possibility of a sociogenic explanation. Such an interest does not ordinarily appear among functionally oriented writers. Talmon developed a psychogenic interpretation of the differential adoption (not existence and elaboration) of the informal tendencies toward exogamy that she so brilliantly describes. Similarly, Coult (1963:275), who also sees the need for a causal analysis, attempts to find it in the "conscious or unconscious recognition of the strains of marriage." The reason why a sociogenic causal explanation has not been considered is simply that the problem, as it has been traditionally formulated, did not encourage it.

Problematic Cases

Yonina Talmon's (1964) analysis of mate selection in the *kibbutzim* is without a doubt the most important empirical contribution to this line of investigation since Murdock's (1949:284) list of eight basic "facts." From the point of view of the solidarity hypothesis, it is especially relevant because it deals neither with a primitive tribe nor a family situation. Her principal finding is that there is an absence of marriages among peer-group members in collective settlements, even though the young people are not related and there are no norms against such marriages. Somewhat harder to summarize is the wealth of material on the attitudes and thinking of the young people. From childhood on, they rarely think of sex or marriage in the context of peer-group activity. Moreover, the attitude of one sex toward the other is one of indifference and, sometimes, positive aversion. Yet young people are attracted to and excited by outsiders, even though courtship has to be secretive.

Her account stresses socializing practices, such as fostering nudity and identical dress, among youngsters in the peer groups, so that no sense of contrast develops. Very likely the process of total identification with the group and suppression of feelings toward particular individuals does start in childhood in the case of incest. Because it begins so early, before the child has the symbolic equipment to understand and manipulate what he hears, learning is unconscious, in the sense of non-verbal; and later in life, he feels a positive aversion and, perhaps, horror at the idea of marriage to an ingroup member, even when—as in the case of the *kibbutz*—the potential mate is not a sibling. But the rather subtle forms that communication to children often takes should not obscure the fact that it is communication, and that what is being communicated is the behavior required to maintain group solidarity. The solidarity hypothesis calls attention to the essential equivalence of these socialization communications with the more general communications about work, defense, ritual, and the importance of the communal attitude in all aspects of life. It calls for a continuation of the analysis beyond the detailed description of one case, to at least an attempt at correlation of the degree of solidarity with the strength of exogamous tendencies in the twelve collective settlements that Talmon studied.

Such a comparative analysis should throw light on the discrepancy between the apparent high solidarity of the *kibbutzim* and the low degree of dramatization of the exogamous tendencies that Talmon actually observed. If a close association is found, we would have to adjust our conception of the range of variation in solidarity and acknowledge that, despite the apparent cohesion in collective settlements, their recent creation and exposure to the cross-cutting influences of a national state keep them from attaining the institutionalized solidarity of some primitive groups.

The second body of case material pertinent to the assessment of the solidarity hypothesis consists of those "exceptions" to the "universal" incest prohibition, namely, the incestuous marriages of the Inca, Egyptian, and Hawaiian aristocracy. Actually, as Middleton (1962) indicates, and as the solidarity hypothesis suggests, incestuous marriages may be much more frequent than we suppose. There must be many communities with such a low level of solidarity that the incestuous unions that occur cannot be effectively sanctioned. The modern tendency is to find such offenders psychopathological, but one wonders whether that label is an adequate substitute for the lack of even minimal social participation in community and in kinship relations.

Although the solidarity hypothesis would predict more frequent incestuous unions in the lower classes, due to greater probability of finding families with extremely low solidarity, even the few cases of aristocratic incestuous marriages repay analysis. Actually, the case material is so scanty and recondite that a detailed analysis must be left to specialists. What is offered below is essentially a sketch of the empirical situation required by the solidarity hypothesis.

It must have been that these aristocratic families, as family units, lacked solidarity. Given the importance of each member—even the children—and the fact that physical facilities and personnel for living as separate entities were readily available, the emotional aversions that reflect common membership in a family group would not obtain. If for instance, a mother reared her daughter in virtual isolation from the father, and assuming that the mother's influence was strong enough to exclude that of the father, the result is essentially two separate families. Chapple and Coon proposed such an interpretation almost twenty-five years ago: "In these cases the royal families have already established relations with other families and other institutions of such a character that the members of the royal families habitually originate to everyone else, and respond in set events to no one. For this reason the parental set has broken down within their families, and it creates less disturbance of equilibrium if they marry sisters or daughters than if they marry outsiders" (Chapple and Coon 1953:302).

This explanation contradicts the one offered by Middleton in his summary of the facts of Egyptian royal marriages. Echoing previous writers, he suggests that brother-sister and father-daughter marriage served to keep the inheritance intact. It is difficult to credit this concern, given the other indicators of disunity. Moreover, it is difficult to see how this explanation would account for the many incestuous marriages among commoners—presumably with less wealth—that Middleton pointedly cites.

What is most problematical about these royal marriages is not that they violated incest taboos present in other sectors of the society, but why they apparently did it so frequently and over centuries. What is suggested is a very narrow field of potential spouses. Very likely they gave the usual rationalization of keeping the bloodline pure, but that is not an explanation. The solidarity hypothesis suggests that each individual was a solidary and therefore "exogamous" unit. Then, applying the hypothesis that requires a concomitant elaboration of endogamy, which in the extreme case defines almost everyone as unacceptable, it is apparent these kings will be positively oriented to their mothers, sisters, and daughters as marriage partners. Still another implication is that these solidary royal individuals would probably not choose spouses from their many female retainers, because these are extensions of the royal person. It is these unions that are incestuous!

FOLKTALES AND SOCIAL STRUCTURE: A COMPARISON OF THREE ANALYSES OF THE STAR-HUSBAND TALE

Abstract: *A powerful method for clarifying theories is to compare their explanations of a particular empirical puzzle. The problem in question is the relationship between the various features of the Star-Husband tale and the social institutions of the tribes in which this story was told. Does the myth mirror the social structure in some way, and if so what aspects of social organization does it reflect? Is it a direct reflection, or is the social reality distorted and perhaps even reversed? Still a third possibility is that both the institutions and the folktale reflect a general structural pattern; and the relationship, if there is one, is between some underlying structural dimension and its diverse social expressions.*

The Star-Husband tale concerns two native girls who, one night as they were sleeping in the open, see two stars. In the composite version that Thompson (1953) gives:

> They make wishes that they may marry these stars. In the morning they find themselves in the upper world, each married to a star—one of them a young man and the other an old man. The women are usually warned against digging but eventually disobey and make a hole in the sky through which they see their old home below. They are seized with a longing to return and secure help in making a long rope. On this they eventually succeed in reaching home.

The adventures of the girl—many stories focus on one girl after she arrives in the sky world—vary with the particular version. In a number of the tales, she dies before she reaches home.

The recent publication of a seventh analysis of the Star-Husband tale opens up the possibility that a comparison of three of the last four, which have much in common, will help to identify the most adequate explanation (Reichard 1921; Thompson 1953; Dundes 1964; Levi-Strauss 1967; Rich 1971; Swanson 1976). The most recent interpretation is Swanson's, who applies his theory of corporate structure and claims that the features of the folktale directly reflect aspects of corporate organization. Earlier, Lévi-Strauss discussed the Star-Husband tale in his *L'Origine des Manières de Table* and proposed that the relationship of myth to reality was a dialectical one, the ultimate purpose of which is to provide imaginary resolutions of social problems. My analysis of the Star-Husband tale followed the alternative route, claiming that the structural dimension of dramatization-solidarity shows up in the institutional features of tribal organization, on the one hand, and the dramatic elements of the tale, on the other. Of the seven analyses, only these three focus on the relationship between myth and social reality. It is true that for Lévi-Strauss the explanation of this link is a secondary concern. As is well known, he is concerned mainly with the internal structure of folktales—what may be called their "algebra"—and in relating this structure to universals of the human mind. Nonetheless, some of his thinking bears on the linkage problem, and it is that line of thought that is reviewed here.

The three approaches share a number of other features. They all treat both the tale and social organization holistically and as group-level phenomena. In other words, the tale is treated as a collective expression and not, for example, as an aggregate, like votes or opinions of the individuals in the society. Second, the analysis of the proposed relationship is either quantified or quantifiable. Both Swanson and Young test their hypotheses cross-culturally and report correlation coefficients in line with the hypotheses. Lévi-Strauss's discussion of the Star-Husband tale is only an illustration of his broader strategy, but his approach may be amenable to some form of quantification. A third similarity is that all the tests or illustrations are static. All three refer to variables of organization that may show change but there is little or no discussion of how the folktales would change in response to shifts in these organizational variables. Very likely the use of cross-sectional data inhibits thinking about dynamics, but adequate explanation demands such a formulation. And fourth, they all claim Durkheim as an intellectual ancestor. This is so despite their divergent interpretations.

Thus, the circumstances are favorable for a conceptual comparison. It is true that a common data set does not ensure that any variation that shows up is due to the differences in the theoretical formulations. Theories always select from data, and even when they focus on the very same item they invariably interpret it differently. But the different interpretations of objectively identical facts provide one important basis for clarifying the theories. If this can be done, of what use would it be? The answer is obvious and fundamental. The clarification of folktale-organization linkages bears on the validity of just about every theory of culture and society, and it is specifically relevant to the many specific links between "text-communications," like speeches, editorials, party platforms, propaganda, soap operas, and grander expressions of "ideology," to the social structure in which they are imbedded. More fundamentally, it would constitute a decisive step in our understanding of "the genotype-phenotype" problem in social structure. It is widely thought that mythological expressions have both a surface and an underlying structure, and a similar claim can be made for the features of social organization. Showing a linkage between folktale and organization would almost certainly throw light on this second problem.

The Folktale as a Direct Reflection of Corporate Organization

Swanson's interpretation of the Orpheus myth is easier to understand than his treatment of the Star-Husband tale, so it may serve as an introduction to the latter. The Orpheus stories told among the American Indian tribes resemble the ancient Greek myth of a man who follows his wife or close relative to the world of the dead and attempts to bring her back. The rulers of the dead agree to release her, but they set conditions, such as forbidding him to look back at his wife on the return home. In other versions, he is not permitted to touch her or return too swiftly. In many of the North American Orpheus tales, the husband disobeys the injunction and loses his wife forever.

Swanson claims that all important tales or myths reflect the problems of corporate organization, that is, organization of a kind that involves decisions for the group as a whole. The main characters of the tale symbolize corporate tendencies, and the dynamics of the plot reflect the strains that are present in different arrangements. Specifically, Swanson (1976) proposes that the husband in the Orpheus story is task leadership in a society, the wife is social-emotional leadership, and the first major movement in the story is an initiative through task leadership to revivify the activities that care for the inner unity of society, when that unity has been weakened or has died away.

This global interpretation of the myth is linked to social organization, by first identifying which societies have institutionalized tasks and social-emotional leadership roles. Any society that is organized for definite collective action will have these roles. The second crucial variable of social organization is the extent to which other aspects of organization work against the articulation of these two functions.

According to Swanson, decision making of any type other than his most simple category ("individuated heteronomy") involves corporate action sufficient for task and emotional leadership roles; therefore, this one variable (that is, individuated heteronomy versus all other types) should predict the presence of the Orpheus tale. But because the story also expresses *problems* of corporate organization, another predictor is the presence of any aspect of social structure that fosters individual actions or decisions that get in the way of collective decision making. Empirically, virilocal residence, a hunting or fishing economy, and forms of government that resemble a federal system—thus allowing for expressions of special interests—are additional predictors of the presence of the Orpheus myth.

Swanson's interpretation of the Star-Husband tale is similar to that of the Orpheus story, but focuses on the distinction between corporate organization and collective purposes rather than on the leadership problem. He interprets the woman or women in the Star-Husband tale as signifying corporate organization, while the spirits (the stars in the sky world) are the collective purposes. Swanson's research strategy is again twofold: Find societies that are capable of formulating corporate sentiments and then look at the conditions that support special interests. The indicators of special interests are the same as before, but the predictor of corporate sentiments is all the decision-making types in Swanson's typology *other* than the two simplest types, which are "individuated heteronomy" and "commensal heteronomy." These two types of collectivity, he argues, are not likely to exhibit collective sentiments.

It goes without saying that one must study the supporting theoretical and research reports that are cited in the article in order to understand both the exact meaning of Swanson's typology and his way of characterizing the dynamics of corporate organization. Even so, it is likely that outsiders will have great difficulty in deciding which aspect of the folktale corresponds to a given feature of corporate organization. Swanson's "code" is not that explicit. Putting that problem aside, his approach may be characterized as a strategy of "global congruence." It is global because the folktale taken as a whole is matched to a form of social organization seen as a whole. It involves congruence because the organizational features are reflected directly in the tale. There are no twists, turns, or distortions; the myth is a faithful expression of corporate structure and articulation problems.

The Folktale as Counterpoint to Organizational Problems

Levi-Strauss's interpretation of the Star-Husband tale is based on a comparison of two variants. The first is found among the Crow and the Hidatsa and the second is found in a broad crescent across Canada. Lévi-Strauss claims that these two variants show "inverse symmetry," particularly with respect to the shift in the status of the porcupine mentioned in the story. In the Plains tale he is a supernatural being while in the eastern Canada version it is treated naturalistically. According to Lévi-Strauss, this transformation of the role of the porcupine in the Plains tale is a response to its absence in the new environment.

However, study of Lévi-Strauss's more extended discussion of the folktale-social structure linkage, in his analysis of the story of Asdiwal, makes it clear that the elaboration of a feature of the folktale, as a consequence of the absence of the item in the group's environment, is merely a special case of a more general principle of interpreting folktale emphases as responses to organizational problems, especially conflict. Thus, Lévi-Strauss sums up his interpretation of this aspect of the Asdiwal story as follows:

> All the paradoxes conceived by the native mind, on the most diverse planes: geographic, economic, sociological, and even cosmological, are, when all is said and done, assimilated to that less obvious yet so real paradox which marriage with the matrilateral cousin attempts but fails to resolve. But the failure is *admitted* in our myths, and there precisely lies their function. (Levi-Strauss 1967)

Further on, Lévi-Strauss makes it clear that the myth is not a "representation" of given empirical facts, although it is certainly related to them. The relationship, he says, is dialectical. In some cases, the institutions described in the myth can even be the opposite of those that exist in reality. Whatever the mythological representation, however, the myth may be construed as a complex "speculation," the function of which is to justify the shortcomings of reality and to persuade the members of society that their institutions, no matter how flawed, are at least preferable to the alternatives reviewed in the myth. Thus, the folktale or myth is a kind of snapshot of collective thought, particularly as it weighs alternative institutional arrangements.

Lévi-Strauss's approach is reminiscent of Freudian dream analysis and, at least in these examples, seems to have a compensatory or re-assuring function. The analysis strategy seems to be that Lévi-Strauss first seizes upon a particular emphasis in the myth, such as the treatment of the supernatural being or the elaboration of conflict activity; he then suggests a general interpretation of the tale that builds on the particular emphasis, linking it to some concrete feature of social organization. Lévi-Strauss claims this link shows a "dialectical relationship," but his examples suggest that the meaning of dialectical is much more complex than in the usual thesis-antithesis-synthesis formula. Also, it is not at all clear why he focuses on one aspect and not another.

The Folktale as an Expression of Basic Structure

The interpretations proposed by Swanson and Lévi-Strauss are highly abstract, but they are not formal. Nor do they entertain the possibility that the relationship between social institutions and myth may be construed as alternative reflections of some underlying theoretical dimension. For both of them, it appears that social organization has priority, and the myth is some kind of complex reflex. Why, though, should the folktale be accorded such dependent status? By most definitions of social institutions the stable configurations that show up in collective ex-pression are just as institutional as are patterns of behavior. This standpoint leads one to ask what dimension may be reflected in both kinds of phenomena. The version of structuralism that has guided my own interpretation of the Star-Husband tale postulates five such formal dimensions, but only the first of these, solidarity, has been investigated using the data from folktales.

The empirical research that illustrates the symbolic structural approach to the analysis of folktales can be construed as a complex measurement exercise, because the theory claims that the values of the underlying structural dimensions for a given society should manifest themselves in all types of "data," such as collective verbalizations, ritual, kinship, economic activity—even artifacts. To validate this claim, there-fore, it is necessary to measure a dimension, such as solidarity, on the basis of one kind of data, and then show that the value that was obtained correlates with the value derived from a second kind of data, such as folktales. In the case of the Star-Husband tale, one of the simpler tests consisted of a count of a number of taboos in each story—on the assumptions that the taboo reflected dramatic contrast and that dramatization is an inherent component of solidarity. This count was correlated with a cumulative scale of male solidarity as indexed by items like the following: There is an exclusive male activity, such as secret societies, men's houses, etc.; some aspect of the male activity is ritualized; there is a hierarchy of officers for the activity; and training for warfare is part of the activity. The exercise is identical to the many studies of social class that seek to show that the stratification of a community is expressed equally well by income, occupational prestige, some index of participation in community organizations, or a scale of "level of living," based on artifacts like pictures or furniture in the living room. The only novelty to the present tests is that one scale was based on the data of collective verbalizations and that the correlation was run on the basis of a subsample of twenty-four North American Indian tribes.

As already noted, structural analysis is quite formal. The content of the folktales is important only in deciding whether the formal features of dramatization are present. If one is studying the solidarity-dramatization dimension, one looks for content that reflects mobilization of effort; focused activity and belief; conflict, particularly with some enemy; and, more generally, sharp contrasts of all types. If one is studying differentiation, attention must be given to the number of specialized roles or activities or, in the case of folktales, the number of episodes or sub-plots that may be interpreted as increasing specialization of ideas. Similar rules, all aimed at indexing the formal character of the structural dimensions, could be listed for the other variables. The theory does not attempt to make sense out of the dynamics of the plot except as they can be construed formally. From some points of view this inability to deal with content is a deficiency, but it has the virtue of cross-cultural applicability. Also, the relationship between the measures is always one of direct congruence. This congruence is of the simplest form, in that the dimension is viewed as expressing itself in two different media, so to speak. Consequently, no code is necessary for linking a feature of social organization to a character in the story or to some aspect of the plot.

Conclusion

In a review of this type, it is customary to conclude that one approach is better than the others and that the latter should be discarded. Such a conclusion assumes that each conceptual position has achieved its maturity and no further development can be reasonably expected. It assumes, also, that the approaches can be judged according to common criteria, although that is rarely stated. On the question of maturity, we can only judge theories on the basis of their present development. The possibility of further elaboration is unknown. The second point is more manageable. One useful criterion against which to judge theories is whether they will contribute to a larger and more systematic investigation of the organization-folktale link. It is one thing for their originators to illustrate the theory or to publish a single test, but it is another thing to apply the theories on a large scale.

How adequate are the three conceptual schemes reviewed here? One conclusion is negative. Against the testability criterion, it is unlikely that Lévi-Strauss's approach would contribute. As already suggested, the theory does not provide guidance as to which feature of social structure of the folktale is significant in establishing a correlation. What role, then, does that leave for the Swanson and Young approaches? Both are still quite esoteric and will have to be simplified. But since they have both been interpreted in empirical terms this should be possible. Moreover, they complement each other in their emphasis on content and formal features (of a certain type). In combination, and assuming elaboration, they may be applied to the empirical problem of understanding North American folktales.

RECONCEPTUALIZING THE FOLK-URBAN CONTINUUM

Abstract: *This review and reconceptualization of Redfield's (1941) theoretical framework that guided his test of the folk-urban continuum argues that the two poles of the typology must be treated as separate dimensions. Then urban complexity can be measured from low to high and the basic scale applied to all the* municipios *in Yucatan, including Redfield's communities. The folk end of the continuum is better interpreted as a "nativistic" movement of the type that Linton conceptualized in 1943. This two-part conceptual reworking adapts Redfield's typology for use in contemporary studies of communities and helps to explain their dynamics.*

After ten years of field work, Redfield summarized his research and thinking about the folk-urban continuum in his book *The Folk Culture of Yucatan* (1941), and it was immediately apparent that his study of the social organization of the Yucatan peninsula rejected many of the anthropological research traditions of his day. His comparisons of three communities and a city diverged sharply from the conventional anthropological study of tribal communities. In contrast to the traditional ethnographies, Redfield's folk-urban typology aspired to sociological universality. This is clear from the summary statement of his hypothesis: "The less isolated and more heterogeneous societies are, the more secular and individualistic and are [sic] the more characterized by disorganization of culture" (1941:xx). These were the components of a hypothesized world-wide transition from folk to urban that Redfield proposed to test in Yucatan.

Why study a concept that was popular among sociologists and anthropologists more than fifty years ago, but is now rarely used? It is of historical interest, of course, because his formulation was an original synthesis of well-known typologies and his empirical test merged sociological and anthropological methods. But revisiting older studies often suggests new lines of research. One immediate possibility is to use the urban component of the typology for describing and measuring all the communities of a region like the state of Yucatan. A second reaction to his work reinterprets the folk end of the continuum in terms of Linton's (1943) concept of "nativistic movements" and applies that concept to a wide range of contemporary social movements.

The research and analysis reported here is not a restudy in the sense of returning to the same four communities. Nor is it a test of the original hypothesis. Rather, it is the kind of conceptual analysis that is increasingly frequent in contemporary social research. It illustrates a revised concept by reference to the data on the universe of 105 *municipios* (county-like administrative units) in the Yucatan peninsula. The list of *municipios* includes three of Redfield's communities, but the census-based variables used for this study are not meant to reproduce Redfield's rich portraits. Like his cross-sectional comparisons circa 1934, it compares communities circa 2000 and makes the same assumption that Redfield did in claiming that his cross-sections reflect change over time. But the two comparison strategies diverge in significant ways—as one would expect after so many decades, and given the contrast between intensive field observations and the descriptive statistical analysis of data for the whole peninsula.

Universal Polar Types versus Degrees of Urban Complexity

Redfield's aim in the Yucatan research was to enlarge the conceptual framework that his earlier study of the folk culture of Tepoztlan had only touched on. The Yucatan research was designed to test the applicability of a synthesis of the European "transition" typologies, especially those of Maine (ascription versus contract), Tonnies (*Gemeinschaft* versus *Gesellschaft*) and Durkheim (mechanical versus organic solidarity). His own reconceptualization focused on the consequence of increased urbanization, emanating from Merida, the dominant city on the peninsula. Both Redfield and the European writers believed that their typologies summarized the evolution of societies, but that term was used in the sense of broad transition, not the Darwinian mechanism of variation and natural selection.

As the statement of Redfield's hypothesis indicates, he saw the urban type as having three principal components: secularization, individualization, and the "disorganization" of culture. The first of these, focusing on the sacred end, he defined as follows: "the extent that there is reluctance, emotionally supported, to call the thing rationally or practically into question" (1941:353). A society is individualistic "to the extent that the socially approved behavior of any of its members does not involve family, clan, neighborhoods, village or other primary group" (355-56). The organization of culture was defined as "the extent to which the society may be described in terms of a single–only one–organized body of conventional understandings" (346). Redfield found empirical referents for these concepts in the customs and practices that varied across his four communities, but it is doubtful that this measurement strategy would work on a larger sample, particularly in regions where agriculture diverges from the maize and small herd cattle culture in the middle of Yucatan. A more fundamental problem with these concepts is that casting them as polar types runs the risk of finding communities that manifest both poles simultaneously. Even when the researcher confines the sample to a standard administrative unit, as is done here, it is likely that just as nations can be both industrially complex and nationalistic at the same time, so, too, villages like Chan Kom can be secular in their production organization and sacred in their ceremonies. It is also likely that they are individualistic and group-oriented depending on the circumstances. Using a single dimension with contrasting poles invites such mixed classifications.

The remedy is to separate the poles and treat each one as a variable that moves from low to high. That move would create six variables for Redfield's (imagined) correlation matrix—and a major task of measure-ment. But there is a remedy for that problem, too, which is to focus attention on Redfield's summary concept—folk-urban—and separate those two poles; then, the task is reduced to measuring the degree of urbanization and "folkness." Urban complexity may be defined as the degree to which community organization manifests specialized occu-pations and organizations. With few exceptions (such as premodern China), such differentiation is found in larger more densely populated places, and it is a principal attribute of the social division of labor. The problem of reworking "folk" is more difficult but still possible, as discussed further on.

The Folk Nativists of Quintana Roo

With only eight municipalities in Quintana Roo and eight small "sep-aratist" communities within one of them (Benito Juarez), statistical analysis of Tusik and its neighbors is not an option. What is possible, and primary in this study, is conceptual analysis of the "folk" pole of Red-field's continuum. A starting point is to distinguish between "nativist" and "nationalist" social movements. Nativism is a movement that claims that a better way of life existed in the past and should be reinstated, by force if necessary. A nationalist ideology claims that a better way of life can exist in the future and attaining it often requires a struggle against a controlling power. Wallace's (1956:265) definition of "revitalization" as "deliberate, organized, conscious efforts by members of a society to construct a more satisfying culture" is "nationalist," and a familiar example of nationalism is the mobilization of American colonists in their struggle for independence. In Redfield's Yucatan, "nationalism," which is not limited to the nation-state, is illustrated by Chan Kom, the "village that chose progress."

Linton's essay "Nativistic Movements" (1958/1943) may be taken as the beginning of both sociological and anthropological attempts to understand nativism. He noted that most nativistic movements "have as a common denominator a situation of inequality between the societies in contact," and that "nativistic tendencies will be strongest in those classes or individuals who occupy a favored position and who feel this position threatened by culture change" (1958: 470, 473). Linton was responding to a flood of anthropological accounts of nativistic movements, the prototype of which is the Ghost Dance religion that appeared among the Paiute Indians about 1890 (Mooney 1991/1896:777 ff; Carroll 1975; Kehoe 2006). The prophet Wovoka preached the practice of a ritual dance that he claimed would hasten the appearance of a messiah who would bring back the animals—buffalo, especially. All the dead Indians will live again. The Ghost Dance spread throughout the Plains to at least 37 tribes (Carroll 1975:400).

An explanation of nativism (and nationalism) would generalize Linton's "situation of inequality" by emphasizing the existential threat that is often present. Then, the "capacity/threat" hypothesis becomes: Weak communities faced with an existential threat will embrace nativism while strong communities will become nationalistic. These responses appear because strong communities come to believe that they have the resources to overcome the threat, while weak communities have no alternative but to draw on their past history (including myths) for organizational strength.

Many of the attributes of the "tribal village" of Tusik are simply the lowest end of the urbanization dimension. Characteristics such as small, isolated, non-literate, kinship-based with a sexual division of labor (plus a midwife and a religious specialist) are typical of the lowest rung of the urbanization dimension. By contrast, the distinctive feature that confronted Redfield's assistant, when he went there in 1935 in the guise of a peddler, was Tusik's suspicion of outsiders. Of course, Tusik was still under threat from the Mexican army. The government only gained acceptance for schools by promising *ejido* rights (Hostettler 1995:140). As Redfield summed up the contrast of Chan Kom and Tusik: "The policy of the (Indians of Tusik) with regard to communication with the world of the towns is the reverse of that prevailing in Chan Kom. Chan Kom sought to build a highway to Chichen. Tusik hides itself in the bush" (1941:52).

In the Yucatan context, we are fortunate to have a set of historical studies (Anderson 2005; Bricker 1981; Burns 1977; Dumond 1970; Hostettler 1995; Jones 1974; Reed 2001; Villa Rojas 1977) that describe the eight villages centered on the ceremonial center of X-Cacal, located about 30 kilometers from Carrillo Puerto (renamed from Chan Santa Cruz, the center of Maya resistance after 1850). On the basis of these reports, we can recognize the nativism of this cluster of villages in the now-faded attributes: the ceremonial center and the representation of the cross are sacred; the instructions from the cross (supplied by one of the priests) are considered final; regular reading of a set of sacred texts (the "counsels") that guide the lives of the residents in the X-Cacal group; outgroup hostility toward the Mexican government and its army; guard units that defend the communities and the ceremonial center; military and religious leaders who are often the same men, but with the religious role paramount; strong separatist tendencies; and the goal of reversing the caste structure so that the Indians dominate the *mestizos*. Taken together, these attributes reflect the efforts of community leaders to find a source of organizational strength in the past when there was no outside help to turn to.

The capacity/threat hypothesis, simple as it is, poses the second question: how to define "strong" and "weak" organization. We have Dumond's (1970: 281) characterization that the weak communities have a poorly developed division of labor and weak formal political organization—two attributes that also characterize the "failed state" definition of a nation-state that is unable to discharge its responsibilities. An alternative concept that subsumes these (Young 2012) defines strength as a community's capacity for problem-solving as embodied in three master-adaptive strategies: the application of specialized knowledge to a community-defined problem; institutionalized contestation over alternative options; and, when the first two fail to produce a "solution," mobilization behind a leader and a program that claims to have a better perspective on the problem. Others could be named, but these primordial strategies are the most frequently employed. They also draw on the same European sociological literature that inspired Redfield, because urbanization is institutionalized, specialized knowledge, and mobilization typically involves religious interpretations. (Contestation, a central feature of democracy, appeared later in the political science literature.) The new idea here is that these dimensions of community structure serve as general adaptive strategies.

Summary and Discussion

This analysis and reconceptualization of Redfield's folk-urban typology has proceeded by dividing it into two separate concepts—urban differentiation, low to high, and nativism, low to high. One product of this conceptual work is a scale of urban differentiation for the *municipios* of Yucatan that is applicable, *mutatis mutandis*, to district-level communities in all regions of the world. Another application, this time of the nativism concept, is a more accurate classification of the many backward-looking movements around the world. Anthropologists were the first to recognize this type of movement, and its potential is enlarged by Redfield's example of Tusik. We can now recognize nativism in the Taliban of Afghanistan, the Christian fundamentalists, the Maoists in Nepal and India, and in the reconstruction period of the defeated southern states of the U.S.

It might be objected that this reconceptualization amounts to a capitulation to sociology. What is left of culture? Of course, the original formulation was sociological. Redfield was influenced by his father-in-law, Robert Park, who led the Department of Sociology at Chicago (Wilcox 2004). Secularization, individualization, and even the "disorganization" of culture reflect sociological thought, as does the fundamental idea of a universal transformation from a folk to an urban type of society. Instead of an objection, it might be better to call this paradigm a productive merger of anthropology and sociology. Another version of this objection is that the cluster of indicators for the urban complexity concept simply reflects the increasing diversity of everyday occupations, agencies, institutions, and arrangements typical of cities, which is true. It embodies none of the subtle and detailed fieldwork that Redfield reports. The implication of statistical analysis is that the in-depth study can be dispensed with and the whole process becomes mechanical. It is true that finding a set of indicators for 100 communities leaves little time and opportunity for detailed fieldwork. But that is typical of extensive comparisons that draw on the power of modern statistics. In principle, however, intensive field work could be added to an extensive study, given more resources. Of course, we cannot know whether the indicators that Redfield reported would meet the criteria for state-wide applicability. His field work was confined to the mixed farming area of Yucatan and might not have the same success in the cattle and sisal regions.

The major implication of this conceptual reworking is that the identification of other dimensions of communities may now be possible. Although many such dimensions have been proposed for communities, they are rarely supported by the heuristic demonstration and theoretical depth that Redfield provided. His openness to contradictory data, as reflected in his handling of the negative findings for the secularization of Guatemalan communities that his colleague Sol Tax collected, is exemplary (Redfield 1941:358). He opened the door to continued research in this paradigm, and the reconceptualization proposed here is an example of what is possible.

THE INFORMANT SURVEY AS A METHOD FOR STUDYING IRRIGATION SYSTEMS

Abstract: *Although informant surveys are probably as old as formal organization, the methodology has only recently been codified. In its present form, it consists of a questionnaire administered to one or several general (not "key" or specialized) informants, objective questions about the institutional aspects of the social systems under study, with statistical analysis oriented to explicating group-level properties. As such, it is a low cost and appropriate technique for surveying fifty or more communities, districts, bureaucracies, businesses, or other formal organizations. As is true of all research methods, its capacity is greatly enhanced by harnessing it to an appropriate theoretical frame of reference, and this article outlines one such approach to the study of irrigation systems.*

Research in rural development is beset by a methodological dilemma: case description is imprecise and does not facilitate cumulative research, while the farm/household survey cannot capture the group-level characteristics of socio-technical systems. In most parts of the world, these are the only two alternatives. Elaborating the field procedures or adding official statistics, if they exist, do not fundamentally alter the choice. But a third alternative is now available. As a result of several recent studies, a case can be made for the "informant survey" as an appropriate research methodology for the study of irrigation associations, and, in fact, other social systems as well.

The informant survey is a technique for collecting information on intermediate social systems, that is, units larger than the family and, for the most part, smaller than state governments. In its minimal form, an interviewer asks a single respondent about the social system that he knows, using a questionnaire. The technique emphasizes questions that deal with well-known institutional features of the social system, the kind that almost any competent adult can answer. It avoids specialized or exotic knowledge. For that reason, the technique is referred to simply as an informant survey, rather than a "key" or specialized informant survey.

Informant surveys are probably as old as formal organization. Administrators have always demanded standardized information from their subordinates who deal with the affairs of particular territories or

agencies. It is no accident that the earliest use of the informant survey in
the context of social science research occurred in Africa, where anthropologists serving the colonial office made systematic surveys of tribal
groups. Since then the technique has been reinvented numerous times
and used for a variety of purposes.

A subsequent section will specify the mechanics of informant surveys, but the essence of this technique is that it elicits information
relevant to the study of organizations treated as units. One asks the informant about the institutional features of his community or irrigation
system, such as "Is the water pumped from the river or a lateral?" "What
type of pump is used?" "Are farmers fined for using more than their
share?" The technique is not appropriate for the study of rates such as infant mortality per 1000 births; the average income of the people; or the
number of times individuals go to the doctor. That kind of information,
to say nothing of the details of households and farms, must be gathered
by a household survey.

The illustrations presented in the following section will make these
abstractions more concrete, but even at this point it is easy to see why the
informant survey can be claimed as an appropriate research methodology
for the study of irrigation systems. It makes research possible on the irrigation system as an organization rather than an aggregate of farmers and
artifacts. The standard household survey is strong in capturing the
behavior of the users, but it is almost a hindrance in understanding the
institutional form. Case studies that employ a mosaic of interviews designed to reveal the institutional features and processes of a system aim
in the right direction, but they cannot, by definition, deliver precision in
measurement, nor do they permit the explicit manipulation of the
variables.

Variations in Technique

The definition of the informant survey may now be expanded. It is a
standardized set of questions that treats, primarily, the institutional
characteristics of a social system (alternatively, a "community"), administered to one or several community members, who respond on the basis
of their knowledge and observations. Enough communities must be
surveyed to permit standard statistical analysis, and this analysis should
generate a group-level description and interpretation of the community.
Thus, there are four components to an informant survey: a questionnaire,

an institutional emphasis, the use of informants, and a statistical analysis that contributes to a group-level interpretation. Occasionally, it is convenient to append a "checklist" of items more easily observed than asked about, but that is merely an option and does not change the principle.

The Questionnaire

Informant questionnaires look like any other well-constructed questionnaires. They are organized from the informant's perspective, beginning with straightforward, non-threatening questions; they then move on by easy transitions to interrelated items; and usually end with any sensitive material, such as the personal characteristics and background of the informant that are needed for quality control. They should not require more than an hour of the informant's time, although, like household surveys, they usually run over that. With exceptions, the questions should be precoded and easily answered in terms of yes/no, simple quantities, or choices. Like all surveys, they should be preceded by pretests and accompanied by close editing. Any adequately trained researcher can be expected to perform all of the above steps, and he/she will also do the exploratory fieldwork necessary for constructing the questions and determining the list of possible answers. Critics of questionnaire surveys seem to assume that schedules are written in hotel rooms over a glass of beer. Unfortunately, some of them probably are, but there is no use debating the merits of unsound and shoddy work; the question here is how a well-administered informant survey compares to an equally well-done survey using another technique.

An informant survey should not be used if there is no interest in the group-level characteristics of the unit under study, be it an irrigation association, a village, or a branch of a bureaucracy. But formulating questions about organizational characteristics is not, it appears, an easy task. Most investigators get off to a good start, by asking about the presence or absence of schools, churches, retail establishments, and, in the context of irrigation associations, the types of equipment, arrangements for maintaining them, the formal organization of the association, and so on. They are usually able to avoid too many questions about the personal characteristics of the leadership or unanswerable questions (using this technique), such as the average wealth of the farmers. The problem comes in formulating questions that get at fundamental dimensions of the organization of irrigation associations and the identification of criterion variables. There are two major reasons for this widespread difficulty. First, the habit of thinking about individuals or households and aggregating them dies hard. Decades of research with household surveys, plus the aggregated statistics of most censuses, condition researchers to such data, particularly when there are few counterexamples of quantitative studies of institutional characteristics. The second reason is related to the first. We simply lack strong theory about significant organizational dimensions.

The question of institutional characteristics is particularly pertinent in the selection of a criterion variable. The most widely used dependent variable is yield of a particular crop, and that is an aggregation of measures generated at the farm level. Even if an informant were capable of making an estimate of the average yield, the basis of the variable is still the farm, not the irrigation association. The same point holds for a number of other important criteria, such as average income, yield variability or any of the many proxies for individual or family welfare. The informant survey is not adequate for producing these estimates, and it is no accident that the two studies described above obtained the estimates from agency records. Apart from that, there is another problem with these criteria, which is that they are not necessarily determined by the efficiency of irrigation. Many other factors, such as market prices, regional organization, ethnicity, etc., are involved; and although these can be investigated, they are not usually considered an intrinsic part of an irrigation survey.

The set of criterion variables that informant surveys can produce coincides with the system problems identified by Coward (1991): water acquisition and allocation, physical maintenance resource mobilization, and resolution of conflicts. These are true system-level criteria, and the construction of indices for these problems would initiate a strong tradition of successive approximation and cumulative research. A reasonable ideal is a family of feasible indicators for each of the four problem areas. It is probably too much to expect researchers to construct a standard set of items, such as those measuring organizational complexity in the Philippines, but that is certainly the goal.

The Informant

The definition of the informant survey stresses the use of a generally knowledgeable member of the community. In practice, one must usually interview the top officer, because part of his job is dealing with outsiders. It is also understood, as already described, that the questions are of general character. They are not the kind of questions that one might ask a specialist such as the pump operator or the extension agent. Separate questionnaires could be administered to such specialists if they are uniformly available. Mixing specialists with general informants is to be avoided, because that will introduce considerable measurement error and undermine the claim of comparability of response. Unlike ethnographic interviewing, the aim is not a multifaceted interpretation based on responses from many different kinds of informants.

It follows from this interpretation of the nature of the informant that the presence of other community members is not a problem. If the questions deal with public facts, then the public should be able to respond to them. It is true that one encounters factions even if the questions seem to be completely general, and we do not as yet have the necessary methodological research to deal with the impact of factional differences. Nonetheless, the problem is not insuperable.

Aside from the number of informants in each community, the other question of numbers has to do with sampling. Sampling is expensive and requires that the interviewers be specially trained to make the correct selections, so it should be avoided if possible. Better to study a small universe. If, in addition, the questionnaire includes questions about the relationships among communities, then surveying the universe is almost a necessity. If one does survey all cases, there is no need for tests of significance conventions, even though it is customary to use such tests as guidelines to the importance of a finding.

Analysis of Data

One would think that this section could consist simply of references to standard textbooks on data analysis and statistics, and to a certain extent this is true. Once the variables have been constructed and checked for reliability and validity (about 50 percent of the work), then the analysis of an informant survey proceeds like any other: cross tabulation, breakdown analysis, correlations, multiple regression, path analysis, and on up the line, whatever is appropriate to the problem. Such advice is correct as far as it goes, but it misses the point of the informant survey. It has already been stressed that this type of survey is appropriate to the description of intermediate social systems, and so the questions should deal with institutional characteristics. It was further noted that these questions should be phrased in the simplest terms, requiring answers like present or absent; a few, many, all; or very important, important, or not important. The idea is to use these limited responses to create an institutional picture.

It is frequently possible to use a single question as an index. If one finds, for example, that the pump operator is compensated in four different ways, then it may not be necessary to ask another question about how the compensation is actually transferred. Single-item variables, however, should be the exception in informant surveys. Instead, the basic rule of analysis with this type of data is that many separate items should be combined into comprehensive indices—"fat" scales, so to speak. The reason for this is that social structure is quite difficult to capture with only one or two indicators. Analysis of the separate items would miss the reality of formal organization, so they must be strung together.

Fact-finding and Preliminary Hypothesis-testing

Although methodology textbooks hold up theory-derived tests of hypotheses as the research ideal, the fact is that a large proportion of surveys in rural contexts are basically descriptive. They start from known characteristics of the social systems under study and attempt to find interrelationships among dimensions that are empirically grounded. They address a wide range of questions that interest practical people. What kinds of penalties are imposed by water users' associations for rule infractions? Have these been increasing in recent years, or do they fluctuate with water shortages? Are there more rule infractions in large systems than in small systems? Are rule infractions more frequent in the perimeters that have higher yield? What about systems that are organized around ethnic groups? These questions are important not only because administrators need answers to them but because they contribute to the factual groundwork that is always necessary to the formulation of abstract propositions.

Fact-finding based on informant surveys has two important advantages. First, it delivers rough but usable quantitative results. The first thing an administrator ought to ask for is the distribution of key variables. Does the size of irrigation perimeters approximate a bell- or a J-shaped curve? What is the minimum and maximum in a given region? After that, it may be appropriate to get to the details. The frequent claim made by ethnographers and case-study advocates that they are able to identify "processes" is usually without foundation. Even if a report did identify an important process, an administrator would be ill-advised to act on such knowledge. One description of a process is rarely adequate in the social sciences; and the steps taken to arrive at such conclusions, from collection of data to the cerebral manipulation of variables, are not open to examination. The results of informant surveys may be more modest, but the procedures are open to verification.

Important as quantified generalizations are, the informant survey holds another advantage that is even more valuable. It forces both the knowledge producer and the knowledge user to become explicit about their concepts. It is simply impossible to write an adequate set of questions about a topic such as penalties for misusing water without fully understanding the phenomenon and extracting the important dimensions. At the receiving end, the administrator is forced to clarify his idea of a problem area, as he looks at the different measures of what usually turns out to be a family of problems. This process of explication goes to the heart of the social science enterprise. Much of what is important in social life is invisible, either because it is intentionally hidden or because we so take it for granted that we are unable to think about it. Explicit questions and rigorously analyzed responses can make social processes visible.

Monitoring and Evaluation

The essence of monitoring is following a criterion variable over time, starting from a carefully established baseline. Evaluation takes up where monitoring leaves off, and it attempts to demonstrate both that an observed change in the criterion variable was in the expected direction and that the change was brought about by at least one particular factor, usually some kind of development program. In the context of irrigation, the standard criterion is usually yields, as these are expected to rise if irrigation technology and organization are improved. To answer the evaluation question, it must be shown that the program is directly linked to the criterion variable and that other possible causes have been eliminated.

The logic of evaluation research is well known and need not be repeated here (but see Young 1985, for an exposition in the context of informant surveys). The question is whether informant surveys can contribute to this type of research. We note immediately that the criterion

variable in irrigation studies is not readily generated by the informant
survey. Estimates of farm-level characteristics are best measured by farm
surveys and then aggregated for purposes of comparing associations.
This deficiency of informant surveys has already been acknowledged;
and one can only add that the farm survey has the opposite problem,
because it is incapable of measuring the organizational features of irrigation systems, which, however, can also serve as criterion variables in
evaluation studies.

So the key question is whether informant surveys are capable of a
degree of accuracy that would permit comparisons of a group-level
criterion, such as conflict resolution or maintenance. At this time, the
answer must be that we simply do not know. We do not have adequate
indicators of such criteria, as we lack knowledge about how fast such
system characteristics change. If they change slowly, then only a very
sensitive index could pick up variation on an annual basis. A reasonable
assumption is that measurement should be made every several years.
Even so, much would depend on the ingenuity and the reliability of the
basic observations. The general experience with informant surveys gives
grounds for optimism that adequately precise monitoring is possible.

SECTION 2
COMMUNITIES

Overview

This section begins with a review of Putnam's book *Bowling Alone* (2000), which was and still is a stimulus to community research. The book underlined a dimension of community organization—participation in voluntary groups—that has been neglected since Tocqueville called attention to it in the 1830s. Reinvigorating community research is quite an accomplishment, but it prompts a question that Putman's book does not answer: the possibility that his index of "civic engagement" is a component of and, therefore, a correlate of socioeconomic status. What we are seeing here is simply a replacement of one component—education—in the socioeconomic (SES) cluster by another—membership in voluntary organizations. Membership may be declining and education increasing, but that shift is by no means the end of the world. Measurement of SES is open to alternative indicators.

As is evident, my analysis of *Small Town in Mass Society* branded it as ideological populism. As such, it is not meant to be tested and, in fact, it is not testable. Like the many varieties of populism that have appeared around the world when times are hard, populist theories in sociology are ubiquitous. This merging of ideology with what is offered as social science will probably continue, because most sociologists are partial to populism. But it would have been gratifying to see a shift in professional opinion once the ideological basis of the *Small Town* book was exposed.

The article on the Goldschmidt hypothesis is the second of three "populist" studies included in this section. All of these were influenced by the folk political belief that "big is bad, and small is beautiful." Many such studies appeared in the post-World War II period, and may have been some kind of reaction to the role of big government in that war. They also reflect a resurgence of materialist ideas (i.e., agriculture and industry as causal) although not the strongly Marxist class-linked kind. Goldschmidt's partner in the Congressional office that employed them during the war was C. Wright Mills, so it is no accident that his research on "branch plants" started with the same populist hypothesis. My counter-hypothesis broke from the "oppressive production organizations controlling small communities" theme of these two papers, by inserting measures of defensive community organization. This move introduced interaction terms and messy statistics, but at least it was on the right track.

The article on regional structure in Africa is included in this section, along with other examples throughout the essays, to illustrate the new methodologies that have been opened up in comparative community research. In this case, coding data from detailed maps makes it possible to compare the regional (mostly provincial) urban hierarchies across sub-Saharan Africa. This use of unusual data for comparisons began in England around 1889, when the religious dissenter Edward Tylor used ethnographic data on a sample of tribes to make generalizations about kinship patterns. It is probably no accident that Tylor was denied an academic position and that Murdock, who codified the method in the form of the Human Relations Area Files, took his degree in sociology. Critics of these comparisons complain that the findings are "thin" and prone to errors, which intensive ethnographic study claims to avoid. But at least the researcher knows how much error a statistical comparison involves. In single ethnographies, errors are buried in the description.

PUTNAM'S CHALLENGE TO COMMUNITY SOCIOLOGY

Abstract: *From time to time in the social sciences, a talented researcher from another discipline comes forth with research and reasoning that reorients a subfield and sometimes the whole discipline. In this essay, I claim that Robert Putnam has probably accomplished that feat for community sociology. I analyze Putnam's two major theses—the decline of community and the explanatory power of his measure of "civic engagement"—and conclude that, although the former is problematic, the latter has great potential for community research.*

Sociologists have been exposed to so many versions of the decline of community that it is a wonder anyone believes there are any communities left. Communities lost their *Gemeinschaft* in the nineteenth century and continued to lose their virtue throughout the twentieth. Lynd and Lynd (1929) claimed that consumerism was eroding the strong values of Middletown (and, by extension, the whole of American society). Vidich and Bensman (1958) followed up by arguing that big bureaucracy was undercutting the autonomy of small communities everywhere. Putnam is not so sure about the cause of the decline that he reports—although television viewing is a prime suspect—but he is convinced that participation in community organizations has weakened and that the trend is ominous. Putman's claim is backed by a wealth of graphs and percentages; the earlier studies simply assumed a past golden age.

In a fascinating appendix to his book *Bowling Alone* (2000), Putnam displays 40 graphs that show some kind of decline starting about 1960. The indicators cover fraternal organizations, business groups, women's groups, children (4H and Scouts), ethnic and religious groups other than churches, sports (bowling receives special treatment), and the professions. I am convinced that decline is evident in a wide array of indicators that most sociologists would accept as "community participation." Beyond that, however, I have some problems.

As Putnam notes, most of the graphs also show a steep ascent beginning around 1920, before the turning point is reached. Some of the declines begin as early as 1940, but by 1960 almost all are moving down. (The sole exception, Veterans of Foreign Wars, will be discussed later.) By 1999, approximately half (eighteen, by my count) had declined to or near their original starting levels.

It is immediately apparent that the word *decline* does not do justice
to the evidence of the graphs. What we are seeing, to borrow a stock-
market analogy, is a "major market correction." But the trouble with that
analogy is its optimistic assumption that these "stocks" will still be
around when the future upturn occurs. Yet many of these associations
will certainly die out. This fact suggests another stock-market analogy: a
shift in the "leading sector." That analogy, in turn, poses a question:
What is the sociological equivalent of the new "technology shares" that
we should be watching for?

Ever since Putnam published his original article (also titled "Bowling Alone"), critics have argued that his data are interpreted more ap-
propriately as transformation. The old-style clubs and associations may
be dying out, but all sorts of new organizations are taking their place. For
instance, networks of "soccer moms" are replacing the weakening PTAs,
and people are engaged in more informal activities. With his new data
sets, Putnam is in a position to reject these alternatives because it appears
that most of them also are in decline. Social visiting, card playing,
neighboring, picnics, and the like (standardized by population) have all
declined. Even the family evening meal is less frequent. And the soccer
moms? After a sharp increase in youth soccer in the 1980s, participation
slowed in the 1990s.

What kind of participation, if any, has increased? "Homeowners
associations" have grown rapidly, especially in California. These
condominium associations vary widely in their performance, but the
organizational format is flexible enough to span Eco Village in Ithaca,
New York, and the Watergate in Washington, DC. Another type that
seems to be expanding is the ethnic or minority identity group. It is
difficult to determine whether these groups have generated actual clubs
and associations, but ethnic "nationalism" is surely a new force in
people's lives, as is feminism. Some of these new communities are
difficult to detect. In New York State a new entity, the "census designat-
ed place," came into existence about 1940; these places numbered 358 in
1990. They are mostly suburbs with no legal status, but they have names
and shopping centers, and people identify with them to some extent. Are
these enough to rejuvenate "community"? We do not know. Still, it is
evident that these are new types of communities, not merely associations
within communities.

A different type of organization is the nationwide interest group,
such as the thousands of Harley-Davidson owners who rally annually in

Sturgis, North Dakota; the Nash Metropolitan and Edsel owners; or the alternative agriculturists. Almost all of these hold local meetings or gatherings, and they stay in touch via the Internet. The same is true of the increasing numbers of professional associations. These organizations have two features that differentiate them from the central office/local branches listed by Putnam. First, they are not so strongly segregated by ethnicity and status. After all, if you own a Harley, what else matters? And second, they depend much more strongly on college-educated people with a national perspective. These new organizations reflect the continuing reinvention of America that the Sixties initiated. They are much more open and fluid; thus it is difficult to see this type emerging. The larger point is that if Putnam, in fact, has documented the decline phase of a transformation, some time must pass before we see the outlines of the replacement organizations.

This brings us to the rise of evangelical religion in America. Putnam does not include churches in his set of graphs, but he devotes a chapter to "religious participation." There he reports the almost certainly inflated survey results that claim 62 percent of Americans considered themselves members of churches in 1980, and that virtually everyone claims to believe in God. He then presents his now familiar graph, which shows a rise in church membership until about 1960 and then a gradual decline, though the decline is less than for clubs. From this he concludes that American church participation conforms to the overall pattern for voluntary organizations, which is reasonable in view of the voluntary character of most churches in the United States. Putnam grants that the fundamentalist churches have increased their membership, but he doubts that they are equally relevant to his concept of "civic community." Quoting various specialists in religion, he notes that evangelicals confine their social activities to the church group, in contrast to the mainline congregations, who participate in the wider community.

A stronger argument for excluding the fundamentalist churches from Putnam's list of replacement candidates is made in books such as Kepel's *The Revenge of God* (1994), which describes a worldwide fundamentalist resurgence. These pathologically conservative move-ments are "nativist" in the sense that they seek to return to what they imagine was a purer and simpler era. This retreatism is a defense against loss of ground in a society that seems to be expanding technologically and economically. Nativism is well known in politics, and it character-izes the activities of the many paramilitary groups in the United States,

who are fanatical about their right to bear arms and even to secede, in
order to form a separate nation. This interpretation would account for the
continued growth of the Veterans of Foreign Wars, the only success story
in Putnam's graphs.

Nativistic movements typically appear as a reaction to a "pro-
gressive social movement" that wins adherents on a broad scale. Putnam
acknowledges that the social movement(s) of the 1960s and 1970s
exerted an effect on most American communities, which is "hard to
overstate," but he does not seem to follow out the implications of this
assessment. Is it a coincidence that the beginning of this Sixties movement coincided with the downturn in social participation? Did one cause
the other? Simultaneous inflections in a wide array of graph lines usually
require a macro event for explanation. Robert Fogel's (2000) recent
exposition of what he calls the "Fourth Great Awakening" elaborates part
of this thesis; it is evident that the macro interpretation could clarify
Putnam's findings.

Putnam's Magical Measure of Social Capital

Putnam first deployed his "civic engagement" variable in *Making Democracy Work* (1993), a comparison of the "institutional performance"
of Italian regions. He introduces a similar measure (now called "social
capital") in this book, which he applies to the fifty American states. In
five "so what?" chapters, he summarizes numerous studies, as well as his
own analyses, which show a strong association between his civic
engagement measure and an array of social indicators that measure
health, happiness, crime, children's welfare, and even the propensity to
engage in fist fights. In addition, Putnam argues that civic engagement is
relevant to enhanced performance of institutions such as schools,
politics, and the economy. Even tax collection is more efficient when
civic engagement is strong.

On this account, Putnam claims that civic engagement improves a
wide array of individual and institutional indicators, even when appropriate variables are controlled for. In the book on Italy, he was satisfied to
show that civic engagement correlated with his 12-item factor score of
institutional performance. In *Bowling Alone*, although he has access to
both institutional and individual-level indicators, he does not build an
index for institutional performance; nor does he take the next step and

analyze its role as a process that intervenes between civic engagement and individual welfare.

What exactly is Putnam's independent variable? Of the 14 items in his index, eight refer to personal participation, such as volunteer services, or leadership in associations, or voting; two refer to informal sociability; and another two refer to beliefs about trust and honesty. Two additional indicators measure the number of associations. All told, 12 of these items take the form of aggregated individual behavior or beliefs. For this reason, as well as for clarity, I refer to the index as a measure of civic participation, in contrast to Putnam's "social capital." Whatever it is called, it has the potential to measure social systems at all levels, from the family to the nation-state, and to predict and perhaps explain a wide array of social indicators. If that promise is fulfilled, it will be an event in the history of sociology.

According to Putnam, civic participation "works its magic" in three ways. First, it allows citizens to resolve collective problems more easily. High levels of trust and citizen participation, the core of social capital, enable people to overcome the inertia and "free riding" that impede collective action. Second, social capital "greases the wheels" that allow communities to advance smoothly. In the economist's phrase, it cuts transaction costs. And third, social capital widens our awareness of the many ways in which our fates are interlocked. In particular, membership in social networks affects members' personalities. People develop character traits such as tolerance, they become less cynical, and grow more empathetic about other people's problems. Putnam seems to accept the reductionist explanation that is now dominant in social epidemiology, when he asserts that psychological and biological processes link social affiliation to improvement in physical health. With this third process, it seems that Putnam is enlarging the definition of "social capital" beyond the originally implied role of facilitating collective action. Now, it appears, social capital helps to improve people's character and health. This third process seems to suggest that social interconnections produce valuable individual-level attributes, and that two of these attributes, trust and participation, generate the networks that continue the process.

Putnam's model, which draws on Almond and Verba's (1963) "civic culture" tradition, is grounded in individual behavior, which builds up the "social." This perspective somehow must resolve the "aggregation problem" of explaining how individual characteristics come to be organized in ways that we call "institutions." Putnam sidesteps the question that would test this perspective. If participation causes longer life, and participation has declined, why has life expectancy in the United States increased steadily since 1900? The graph line for life expectancy (Zopf 1992:231) shows fluctuations until about 1945, followed by a near-plateau from 1955 to 1965, but then the curve moves up again. How can this be? Putnam presents evidence that people's self-rating of health has been declining, but he does not show the objective evidence. Does the structural approach have an answer? Not yet, but it should be able to show that, despite the decline in conventional social participation, social problem-solving capacity at all levels of communities has increased. We do not yet know what these new problem-solving mechanisms will turn out to be, but research might begin with those television programs, even the sitcoms, which Putnam disregards.

SMALL TOWN IN MASS SOCIETY REVISITED

Abstract: *The case study of a small New York town that dramatized the thesis that the secular expansion of macro forces—urbanization, industrialization, and bureaucratization—has permanently reduced the autonomy of all small communities is an example of a special type of discovery/persuasion strategy in the social sciences: the "opposition case study." In contrast to the more rigorous "competitive test" or the theoretical "negative case," opposition case studies confront the dominant perspective with a qualitative illustration of a new theory in the context of a zero-sum game. When they are successful, opposition cases meet four criteria: the dominant view is immediately rendered obsolete; the origin of the new idea supports its plausibility; the new perspective is shown to be testable; and the new perspective quickly generates new lines of research.* Small Town in Mass Society *meets the first criterion, and may have been heuristic, but its probable origin in populist ideology undermines its testability.*

In 1958, two sociologists, Arthur Vidich and Joseph Bensman, published their study of a New York township and village, and concluded that the residents were "powerless in the face of the domination they experienced by agencies and institutions of the larger society" (1958:ix). This statement summed up a more general theoretical perspective that asserted the increased control by "mass society" over the decisions made in small communities, thereby repudiating the conventional view that small communities represented a distinctive way of life. In their introduction to the 1968 edition, Vidich and Bensman looked back on the previous ten years and concluded that "students of the community are now able to study the community within the framework of large-scale, bureaucratic mass society rather than as the polar opposite of urban society" (1958:vii).

By 1994, *Small Town* had sold more than 90,000 copies. It was revised in 1968 by adding new material and some previously published articles, and for many decades it was a favorite monograph for undergraduate classes in community. At the same time, professionals, at least as reflected in reviews, accepted its main conclusions with little or no question. Statements such as "the net effect . . . has been that all rural localities become less autonomous and more dependent" were offered without a question mark (Hobbs 1995:386; Allen and Dillman 1994;

Gallaher 1980). This widespread acceptance of the thesis that small town democracy "had no basis in fact" poses an important question in the sociology of knowledge and for the status of scientific method. Why was such a view, so at odds with the conventional picture of small communities, so readily accepted? What were the sources of this new perspective?

This essay analyzes this and similar questions by asking the generic question, Is *Small Town* an example of a well-known genre in social science, the "opposition case?" And if so, was it successful? The term "opposition case" here refers to a case study that proposes a theoretical perspective that flatly contradicts the standard view of the problem. The theory is usually so intertwined with the qualitative presentation that it is hard to see clearly, but the whole package is persuasive. Indeed, the history of sociology lists a number of such oppositional case studies: Durkheim's demonstration of the social basis of religion using dense ethnographic data from Australian aboriginal groups; Warner's repudiation of the Marxist class framework by describing socioeconomic status in "Yankee City"; Margaret Mead's claim, in the heyday of anthropology, that culture, not genetics or physiology, shapes human development. Likewise, Kuhn's (1970) outline of how revolutionary change in science is socially grounded confronted rationalist claims for the accumulation of knowledge; and Frank's (1970) essay dramatized how supposedly benign contact with large capitalist economies led to economic stagnation in small, dependent countries.

Does *Small Town* fit this picture of the opposition case? Its thesis that macro forces constrain and circumscribe the small community certainly challenged the then-accepted view that small town culture was independent and that local democracy was the bedrock of American society. The book illustrates a counter-position that may be labeled "bureaucratic dependency." Like Frank's dependency thesis and other opposition case studies, *Small Town* is either/or; and it does not spend much time arguing with the conventional view, it just supplants it. Successful opposition cases are justly celebrated in the history of sociology. How do they achieve this success? Typically, the superiority of the new perspective is established within a few years; certainly no one waits for confirming evidence. Indeed, it is often implied that the new view is so obvious that empirical testing is irrelevant. Such a process appears to account for the success of *Small Town,* and the book thus warrants retrospective analysis. The exercise may help us understand how shifts in perspective are introduced into the literature of sociology.

How can we evaluate this rather specialized strategy? What is needed is a set of criteria that are applicable to the appearance and immediate aftermath of the counter position. One such criterion, already implied, is whether the statement of the opposition position effectively terminates the hegemony of the received position. In other words, after hearing the opposition position, do professionals say, "Why did we ever believe the conventional theory in the first place?"

A second criterion is provenance. Just as art critics establish the origin, in the many meanings of that term, of a painting, a new theory should be contextualized. Theories do not come out of nowhere, even if their authors are ignorant of their theories' origins: there is usually a classical source that suggested the theme, and more recent theorizing may also have influenced its form. Moreover, the political ideas of an era are also quite relevant to the gestation of sociological theories.

A third criterion is testability, a standard requirement of sociological theories that is often difficult to establish immediately, even in principle. Opposition cases may introduce perspectives that require new methods. But professional analysis and judgment cannot be postponed indefinitely. At some point, the theory must be clear enough so that professionals can debate it without overwhelming confusion. Its concepts must at least suggest what kinds of empirical situations should be researched.

A fourth criterion is that the new theory is heuristic. Again, this characteristic of good theories is usually not immediately apparent. Soon after its emergence, however, the theory should suggest other avenues of exploration, applications, interesting implications, and even new branches. Certainly, it should not stifle thought.

Vidich and Bensman's version of the mass society hypothesis focuses on the policies imposed by government and other centers of authority: "Governmental, business, religious and educational super-bureaucracies far distant from the rural town formulate policies to which the rural world can respond only with resentment" (1968:323). They also mention economic pressures, such as the squeeze on local profits that results from franchises or big firm competition, and they refer to the general standardization and uniformity of popular culture, religious ceremonies, and the content of education, but their central theme is increasing bureaucratic control. In this regard, in a later article, Vidich points to bureaucracy as the common denomination of all macro forces (Vidich 1980:125).

   This preoccupation with bureaucratic impact is reflected in a
hypothesis to the effect that "power and local political affairs . . . tend to
be based on accessibility to sources of decisions in larger institutions"
(1968:100). Inasmuch as power holders are motivated to hide the source
of their power, an "invisible government" forms. A key actor in this new
arrangement is the local attorney, a person who is an expert on interpreting externally imposed rules and regulations.
   A second corollary is that the local belief system that celebrates
small town life is a collective buffer, necessitated by the gap between the
local powerlessness and a populist heritage that exalts the small community. Vidich and Bensman elaborate this corollary by formulating the
themes in the local belief system: "just plain folks," local superiority
versus out-group defects, "neighbors are friends," there are good folks
and bad folks, and "we're all equal." As is generally true of small town
populism, there is an antipathy toward big government, which one
resident described as "overridden with bureaucrats and the sharp deal,
fast-buck operator, both of whom live like parasites off hard-working
country folk" (1968:32). Vidich and Bensman compare this small town
ideology to the defensive use of nationalism, tribalism, and anti-
Westernism in parts of the underdeveloped world (also see Padfield
1980). It is important, however, to be clear about the hypotheses that
Vidich and Bensman are not advocating. Although they sometimes sound
as if they believe that macro organization has simply displaced local
functions, they do not argue that position. Rather, they argue that, in
almost every area of jurisdiction, the board has adjusted its action to the
regulations and laws externally defined by outside agencies, which
engage in functions parallel to its own. State police, regionally organized
fire districts, state welfare agencies, the state highway department, the
state youth commission, and the state conservation department—these
agencies and others become central to the daily functioning of the village
(1968:113). While this adjustment process can include cancelling local
functions, as when the town drops the local policeman in favor of the
county sheriff, *Small Town* focused on the qualitative change in politics
forced on small places. Had Vidich and Bensman simply argued loss of
functions, their proposition would have become a tautology: the more the
state takes over local functions, the less the local autonomy, because
autonomy means deciding about local functions.
   Small Town must also be distinguished from "European mass society theory" (Halebsky 1976; Kornhauser 1959), which analyzed the atom-

ization of citizens under systems such as fascism and communism. In such regimes, local government is subverted by the party and the secret police. Of course, Vidich and Bensman may have been influenced just enough by European mass society theory to formulate a weak version of the hypothesis: Local government is limited but not completely subverted by the state and federal bureaucracy. Such a formulation would correspond to the centralized French system that Becquart-Leclercq (1988) describes. But that hypothesis assumes more centralized authority than was ever true for the state or federal governments in the U.S.

It appears, then, that Vidich and Bensman are using the term "mass society" simply as a summary phrase for faceless, ubiquitous macro organization. But their focus on the bureaucratic element is much narrower than, for example, Warren's (1978:52 ff) inventory of the elements of the "great change" that communities have experienced. Warren's list may be divided into the economic, the bureaucratic, and the cultural, but Warren would be the first to concede that there is great overlap among these categories. Vidich and Bensman do not attempt to test the Warren (1978:52) hypothesis that "the 'great change' in community living (is associated) with a corresponding decline in community cohesion and autonomy, especially the reduction of 'horizontal ties'." Their *Small Town* version, parallel but independently formulated, focuses on bureaucratic control. Warren (1978:241-42) mentions "subordination" and "dependent," but he clearly does not mean these in the strong sense that Vidich and Bensman do.

The Provenance of the Mass Society Thesis

Vidich and Bensman do not report the sources of this theoretical framework, even in footnotes. While it is true that community studies rarely cite their intellectual origins, and oppositional case studies may not even have an explicit intellectual framework, this picture of community organization and culture is so distinctive that some indications of the origin of its theoretical framework would have been useful. Nevertheless, their primary concern with the impact of bureaucratization suggests Weberian origins, particularly Weber's characterization of the constraining effects of bureaucracy on society (Weber 1946:224 ff). As is well known, Weber was pessimistic about the impact of "iron cage" bureaucracy on individual freedom. Still, it is worth remembering that Weber had a certain begrudging respect for modern bureaucracy and he certainly thought it was an improvement over the unpredictable patron-client relationships of neopatrimonialism. On that point, Vidich and Bensman's (1968:x) suggestion that U.S. communities are comparable to Third World communities is mistaken. Most Third World communities, then and now, would have been grateful for the stability and even-handedness of bureaucratic regulation. Of course, Weber gave little thought to the impact of bureaucracy on small towns, so Vidich and Bensman appear to be drawing on a populist perspective for their inter-pretation of clique-run local politics and defensive false consciousness. Indeed, their emphasis on the local distortions of thought and action is so marked that it is reasonable to infer influence from the European intellectuals who arrived in the U.S. after World War II, with ideas about the appearance of a standardized, alienated, "one dimensional man." Very likely all of these ideas were "in the air" in the 1950s, and some of these themes appear in Nisbet's (1953) *The Quest for Community.*

A Generalization of U.S. History?

A stylized fact that seems to provide the bedrock for the mass society thesis is the alleged secular shift from local to outside control. As one of the project leaders (with the help of Vidich) summed it up: Much in local organizational life, moreover, has its roots outside the community. The school, though formally under local control, in fact is influenced at every turn by the state, which contributes three-quarters of its support. The churches receive their minister and many of their policies from their national organizations. And the same is true of the local chapters of such national organizations as the Grange and the American Legion. Even the local town and village boards have found their area of sovereignty gradually withering away, as more and more of their functions are taken over by the county and state. Indeed, the principal activity of these local boards today is filling out forms and meeting requirements and deadlines set by state and county levels. The implication here is that local commu-nities were once autonomous.

Tocqueville's account of local government in eighteenth century New England seems to set the baseline for the claim that American towns were formerly independent. Referring to the colonial period, he wrote, "political life had its origin in the townships; and it may almost be said that each of them originally formed an independent nation . . . [T]he kings of England . . . were content to assume the central power of the state. They left the townships where they were before" (1954:67). Tocqueville goes on to qualify this statement: "There are certain duties, however, which they are bound to fulfill. If the State is in need of money, a town cannot withhold the supplies; if the State projects a road, the township cannot refuse to let it cross its territory; if a police regulation is made by the State, it must be enforced by the town; if a uniform system of public instruction is enacted, every town is bound to establish the schools which the law ordains" (1954:68). In view of this significant qualification, it seems more reasonable to suppose that the earliest phase of local independence was an accident of history. What else could the kings of England have done with a population so distant and with so few colonial administrators? Under frontier conditions, autonomous local government would appear spontaneously—until such time as superordinate control could be imposed.

In fact, there is good reason to believe that localities had less autonomy in the past. The U.S. Constitution refers only to the states; and legal opinion, specifically "Dillon's Rule" of 1868, spells out in no uncertain terms that local governments have only the powers assigned to them by the states. Indeed, as a crucial section of Judge John Dillon's decision reads: "Municipal corporations owe their origin to, and derive their powers and rights wholly from the legislature. It breathes into them the breath of life, without which they cannot exist. As it creates, so may it destroy. If it may destroy, it may abridge and control" (Zimmerman 1995:19). This rule has withstood many legal challenges, but in recent decades, according to Zimmerman, states have relaxed their grip on local governments, and New York, in particular, has given communities a great deal of latitude.

True, the process of "unshackling" local governments has been accompanied by the countertrend of mandates. These are legal requirements imposed by the state on local governments, which may cover any local function. Mandates deal with general government, public safety, health and sanitation, highways, social service programs, culture and recreation, education and various unclassified functions, such as a county-owned airport operation, or rules concerning fish and game. A 1978 study found that New York had mandates in sixty out of seventy-seven functional areas, more than any other state (State of New York, 1981:2). Yet most of these new rules were imposed after the Vidich and Bensman study.

In addition to mandates, superordinate governments may pass laws that "preempt" local laws. A publication by the U.S. Advisory Commission on Intergovernmental Relations (1992) tabulated the number of such preemptions of state and local authority by the federal government, and it concluded that beginning in the 1970s, there was a sharp rise in the number of such statutes. This high level continued through the 1980s and was projected through the 1990s. But the 1950-59 decade, during which Vidich conducted his fieldwork, had a much lower level of such statutes. Its count of twenty-seven such laws was an increase of only about ten over previous decades. The twenty-seven preemptions covered civil rights, health, safety in the environment, commerce and transportation, and banking, finance, and taxation, though none of these categories showed anything but proportional enlargement. These figures suggest that, while there may be justification now for thinking that there are too many federal regulations, there was little or no justification in the 1950s, when Vidich and Bensman wrote their book.

This claim of a secular shift deserves closer analysis. In the first place, there is no thought that it represents an authoritarian situation, where a representative of the state resides in the town and effectively rules. Indeed, except for the requirement to submit various reports to the state government, there is little contact. Second, there is still considerable local decision-making by any standard; what is at issue is the objective/perceived increase in state control. Third, the local population elects its leadership and presumably could elect people with more skill in resisting state laws. Such local choice also operates with respect to ministers and school officials, who can always be forced out. With respect to doctors, agricultural representatives, and supermarket managers, the residents can simply vote with their feet.

One last set of facts is relevant to the origins of this hypothesis. According to a survey completed in 1952, there were thirty-three separate organizations in "Springdale," not counting the twenty-five church or church-related groups. "These organizations account for between 2,500 and 3,000 organizational memberships—an average of one or two per Springdale adult" (Goodchilds and Harding 1960:26). In other words, Springdale was a highly organized community, almost certainly the best organized among the nine towns of the county. Is this level of participation consistent with objective "powerlessness?" All experience suggests that people who participate in one way participate in others. Of all the places that Vidich and Bensman could have chosen to illustrate their thesis, this must have been the worst. How could they have found powerlessness in a community such as that? Vidich and Bensman would surely reply that these figures actually prove their point about outside control, because all these clubs reflect centrally formulated programs. This reversal of conventional opinion dramatically illustrates Kuhn's claim that paradigm changes are fundamentally gestalt shifts.

Is The Mass Society Hypothesis Testable?

Oppositional case studies are not designed to prove hypotheses, so a discussion of how the proposition could be tested may be considered irrelevant. On the other hand, the logic of proof must eventually be imposed, so it is useful to look ahead. Such an empirical preview also tells us a great deal about the meaning of the hypothesis. As Vidich and Bensman describe the process in Springdale, it is clear that they believe that small towns, as a category, suffer from bureaucratic dependency. State laws may allow for some exceptions, and there is certainly variation in administration, but the mass society hypothesis is fundamentally categorical. Consequently, a comparison group must be a different category of community. In fact, Vidich and Bensman suggest that small towns should be contrasted with cities where, according to these authors, urban dwellers react to the problem of outside control by the cultivation of privacy, leisure, and culture (1968:x). These "defenses" are not comparable to small town populism, because cities cannot draw on that tradition. Their situation also is different in another respect, according to Vidich and Bensman: City dwellers share the same geographical and cultural milieu as the dominating agencies.

The *Small Town* hypotheses imply a longterm bureaucratic expansion of the state and federal governments, which must be shown to have a uniform impact on all small towns (see Richards 1978). On the basis of their reference to populism, we may infer that Vidich and Bensman were thinking of a time span of about 150 years. What could one use for a control group for such a period? A longitudinal study of a few towns might work, but a shorter time line of fifty years would probably serve most purposes. Vidich and Bensman do not entertain this possibility, so it is unclear how long the process takes. Apart from the difficulties of designing a test of this type of change hypothesis, a number of conceptual problems raise the question of whether it involves so much ambiguity as to undercut any attempts to test it. Had Vidich and

Bensman simply proposed a special case of the "great change" hypothesis, such as "The greater the expansion of state bureaucracies, the more likely it will be that small town politics will be oriented to their policies," the test would have been difficult enough. But to claim that bureaucratic control causes local dependency and pathologies such as backroom political manipulation and defensive ideology is pushing the limits of empiricism. While it is true that all hypotheses involve preconceptions and value judgments, some are so ambiguous that trained professionals can never agree on a test.

The characterization of bureaucratic impact in *Small Town* raises the question of whether the general causality the authors assert is possible. Their examples are random: There are rules for the dairy farmers, the local government is constrained by a different set of rules, and the policies of churches and clubs affect people in other ways and at different times. Can all these be bundled together and conceptualized as bureaucratic control? How could one theorize a uniform impact from such disparate events that vary in meaning from group to group, depending on context? How many sectors must be affected to reduce autonomy? How does one identify and count sectors? Does local government count as one or does an imposed zoning regulation count as one? Even if we assume that all the institutions of the community become "branch plants," so to speak, doesn't the community as a political unit keep its autonomy? Again, however, Vidich and Bensman have a reply. It is precisely this disparity of outside control that undermines community unity. Community sectors are pulled in opposite directions, making coordination impossible. What, then, is a reasonable level of autonomy for small communities such as villages and townships? Complete autonomy is impossible so long as the community is part of a state or federal system. In the United States, at least, local autonomy equivalent to that enjoyed by states is probably the upper limit, but one not likely to be attained. The next level down would be "home rule" within a framework set by the state and federal government. Cross-cutting this dimension of autonomy is the legal definition of administrative levels and the allocation of appropriate responsibilities. Local governments in New York State seem to fit the middle level, and they did so in 1950.

Nowhere in *Small Town* do we find a clear exposition of the intervening processes that link bureaucratic control to outcomes such as backroom government and defensive ideology. Specification of an intervening process is a minimum requirement of an adequate hypothesis; omitting it typically masks a tautological claim. We need to understand why the local elite took the trouble to work behind the scenes. Vidich and Bensman say that the town fathers were "stingy and anal" (1968:320), concerned only with keeping taxes low, but if they were, they must have had many supporters, and they could have come out publicly. Perhaps they are postulating a general tendency for power brokers to hide their negotiations. Moreover, it is interesting that Vidich and Bensman did not mention the general paternalism that probably characterized local leaders of that era.

What about the defensive populism? That seems to require a complex psychological process that begins with some degree of recognition of dependence, followed by a nativistic appropriation of populist rhetoric. Then the process would have to be duplicated in the minds of enough residents to become a community-wide orientation. In the 1950s, such reductionist psychodynamic processes posed no problem for theorists, but now we see that they involve the aggregation problem: How were all these individual reactions transformed to a shared belief system?

Then there is the problem of overt bias. Like the dependency writers who followed them, Vidich and Bensman pepper their description with words like powerlessness, domination, resentment, and self-deception. The "surrender of jurisdiction" is managed by "alien experts," while the voluntary contribution made by the local lawyer to the work of the village board is described as an example of domination by an "unelected expert." All this leads to "political paralysis," control by the "invisible government" and dependence on "extra-legal bodies." Insofar as these terms reflect the general text, and they appear to do that, they suggest a populist ideology that is not testable, nor is it meant to be tested—except possibly in the political arena.

Has the Small Town Thesis Been Heuristic?

Conceptual fruitfulness takes many forms. Almost certainly, *Small Town* made it easier for students of community to take the macro environment into consideration. Although our literature review uncovered no such studies, it is easy to see how *Small Town* could have provided a framework for the study of state-local relations, particularly local reactions to newly imposed regulations. Likewise, research on community politics was probably stimulated, even if researchers were not able to find many "invisible governments."

Small Town did stimulate, directly or indirectly, a number of alternative explanations of changes in small town structure, and this is another kind of fruitfulness. Only four years after *Small Town* appeared, Edward Shils (1962) responded to the challenge posed by mass society theory. For Shils, "mass society" is better interpreted as referring to "a new order of society which acquired visibility between the two world wars" (1962:47), and which facilitated the integration of the mass of the population. The macro expansion of the interwar years exemplified a much higher degree of vertical integration. Government became more responsive to local requests and demands, and the local populations became much better educated and informed by the mass media. The populace accepted the authority of the major institutions of society and responded in a responsible and participant manner. Shils believes that a conception of mass society, where power takes the form of manipulation, repressing civic spirit and erasing individuality, is a gross distortion of liberal-democratic societies.

According to Shils, the new type of mass society is a consensual society, but with plenty of room for the conflicts of democratic pluralism. Despite the internal competition, there is "more of a sense of attachment to the society as a whole, more sense of affinity with one's fellows, more openness to understanding, and more reaching out of understanding among men" (1962:51). Every human being is a participant in this more strongly integrated society, and language binds them together. Objectively, mass society is also a welfare society; it is an industrial society (an attribute that enhances integration); it is a bureaucratic society (which delivers services according to impersonal and universalistic standards); and given its large size, it is necessarily a pluralistic society.

Shils' essay is broadly conceptual in the grand tradition of social thought. He draws his illustrations from history and society at large; there are no references to empirical studies. If one were to undertake such a study, it would probably come off as a positive version of *Small Town*, because Shils' framework gives little guidance for comparisons of communities. Nor would it serve as a true counter-hypothesis, for it accepts the mass society framework; the difference is that Shils judges the effect as positive.

A more recent study that implicitly rejects the control thesis of *Small Town* is Putnam's (1993) claim, based on a comparison of Italy's regions, that "civic community" (as measured by voluntary organizations, newspaper readership, and voting), is the key variable that accounts for government performance. Putnam does not mention control by the central government. Indeed, it is easy to see how this local, capacity perspective could be elaborated upon, by adding other capacities and by dropping "outside pressures" entirely, on the grounds that they are heterogeneous and constantly changing and, therefore, they could not be the cause of anything like democratic stagnation.

Vidich and Bensman need not have waited for Shils and Putnam to see the most obvious alternative to their interpretation. Part and parcel of modern, multilevel government is the allocation and, if the circumstances require, the reallocation of functions to the different levels. That is, since the Roosevelt era, government has taken on a broad range of new functions. The modern state is now concerned with public health, welfare, and economic development. In New York, the counties manage most of the health and welfare functions, but "development" efforts, from attracting business to subsidizing public housing, is a concern at every level.

Again, however, Vidich and Bensman have a reply. While it is certainly true that the assigned duties and responsibilities of one level of government "limit" those of subordinate levels, and local governments must debate and respond to laws and policies imposed by higher levels, the point of the mass society hypothesis is that multilevel organization has become top-heavy, bearing down on local organization in ways that threaten the local identity (Vidich 1980:126).

Nonetheless, the multilevel framework leads to a consideration of the interrelations of administrative levels and the determinants of local self-determination. This perspective assumes, first, that the macro-micro dichotomy of mass society theory is an oversimplification. It therefore substitutes a multilevel framework that makes room for counties, metropolitan regions, and an explicit state government. Second, it assumes that the levels are defined in both legal terms and in empirical reality, and that the goal is to identify their stable structural attributes, such as the degree of professional specialization or of administrative pluralism. Third, the multilevel framework accepts, at least as a start, the mass society hypothesis of downward causal direction, but it quickly moves on to the reciprocal relations and the possibility, following Shils, that some superordinate structures actually enhance local autonomy.

This review of alternatives to Vidich and Bensman's bureaucratic dependency interpretation underscores the fact that almost all of them (Putnam is the exception) have accepted the macro-micro frame of reference; no one has proposed a return to the rural-urban continuum. But the various hypotheses are not examples of "fruitfulness" in the usual meaning of that term. Rather, they are alternatives to the Vidich and Bensman version. On the other hand, *Small Town* is consistent with multilevel thinking, and it is heuristic in this area.

Evaluating Opposition Case Studies

In the introduction of this essay, the "opposition case" strategy of dis-covery and persuasion was intentionally defined as the presentation of qualitative evidence in support of an iconoclastic position, because that is the form it usually takes in the social sciences. Quantitative and experimentally designed counter positions are best called "competitive tests," and are favored in the more mature sciences. Also excluded are "negative cases," such as Oscar Lewis' (1951) restudy of Tepotzlan or Freeman's (1983) restudy of Margaret Mead's Samoa, neither of which introduced any new theory. It should be clear, also, that the meaning of "opposition" is that of a zero-sum game: If one theory is correct, the other must be wrong. How does the bureaucratic dependency opposition case measure up against these criteria? Certainly, rural-urban advocates were immediately put on the defensive. Suddenly, the dominant view seemed static and lacking in causal structure. It ceased to be interesting. Very likely, the rural-urban continuum had outlived its usefulness in any case. Like the "special creation" belief that Darwin challenged, it had become more of a verbal convention than a serious theory. Nevertheless, it takes a counter position to clear the air, and *Small Town* accomplished that task.

Did *Small Town* have a provenance that supported its credibility? Here the judgment is negative. If the origin of this thesis is in Weber, then it is a misreading of his thoughts on bureaucracy. If it is a conceptualization of the facts of U.S. history, then the facts do not support such a thesis. Where did the idea come from then? One interpretation is that Vidich and Bensman somehow sensed the *leitmotif* of dependency theory and formulated an earlier version of it, including its populist suspicion of authority. In a later article, Vidich explicitly echoes the populist persuasion: "By this mechanism (blaming foreign control of technology), the resentment against the dominant institutions . . . can be expressed directly either against the hated foreigners who live within the community or against the seats of central government and multinational corporations within the metropolitan society itself" (1980:127).

Although, "populism" has many meanings (Canovan 1985; Kazin 1995), its core theme is the resistance of plain people to an array of large, hostile forces. True, most populist rhetoric emphasizes the economic— small producers resisting big business—but Vidich's idea of "bureaucratic forces" is consistent with the central theme. It is also true that Vidich does not refer to any evil intentions of the bureaucrats—for him, bureaucracy is impersonal. Essentially, Vidich and Bensman have converted the local populist perspective into a general hypothesis.

Is this version of the mass society thesis testable? An immediate challenge is the design problem introduced by the categorical form of the hypothesis: All small towns are made powerless. That form makes finding a control group difficult, if not impossible. The hypothesis would have been easier to manage had Vidich and Bensman allowed for variation, as dependency theory did, but that is not possible here because the bureaucracies are state- and even nation-wide. One could count the number of "branch establishments" in a community, but such a count would be extremely ambiguous.

The real question concerns conceptual clarity. It is disquieting to read references to "mass society" followed by a phrase, "whatever that might be" (Johansen and Fuguitt 1984:205). The clearest idea of what is here labeled "bureaucratic dependency" seems to be the claim that the imposition of policies from the central offices automatically delimits democratic self-determination. But is outside "control" an automatic outcome when the residents have a veto power? If control/dependency is intrinsic to outside policies, where is the causal, as opposed to the tautological, proposition? It is almost as if Vidich and Bensman wanted to avoid formulating a testable proposition. Indeed, when one considers the implication that only isolated groups, like the "shack people," are autonomous—an obvious sociological absurdity—it seems that we are dealing with a Sixties-type ideology, and not sociology.

Was it heuristic? There appears to be no tradition of "bureaucratic dependency" studies per se, but the general thesis did provoke a number of counter perspectives and explanations. Insofar as it contributed to the reception of a broader multilevel framework, its influence must be judged as positive. Such a framework would complete the gestalt shift that *Small Town* initiated. On the negative side, there appears to be no elaboration of bureaucratic dependency per se. What seems to have happened is that the bureaucratic dependency thesis has stifled research on the community (Summers 1986:349). If communities are puppets of macro forces, why bother with them?

In this context, the fate of A. G. Frank's (1970) zero-sum version of economic dependency theory is instructive. Despite the initial success of Frank's thesis, few would now insist that large capitalist countries systematically exploit dependent economies, leaving them all stagnant. It is noteworthy that Cardoso and Faletto (1979) published their more moderate interaction interpretation of trade and development less than a decade after Frank's iconoclastic essay. *Small Town* appears to be following the path of Frank's essay: initial success followed by the realization that it is ideological, in the sense of containing a fundamental ambiguity that must be taken on faith. It is best understood as an implicit elaboration of American populism. Why were the problems in *Small Town* not noticed earlier? The answer has already been implied in our label "bureaucratic dependency." *Small Town* was a precursor of economic dependency theory and rode that groundswell. But that judgment introduces another criterion: "resonance" with the "tenor of the times." Many opposition case studies seem to echo a generalized wave of thought, and this relationship of ideas to culture has often been noted. But it cannot serve as a fifth criterion of opposition case success; assessment of such a complex relationship is probably beyond our capacity at the present time.

THE GOLDSCHMIDT HYPOTHESIS IN CHILE

Abstract: *The claim that large farms with hired labor undermine community institutions and reduce average welfare while family farms enhance these dimensions is tested in the context of Chile's expanding large-scale export agriculture. The expected negative effect of scale shows up statistically but then disappears when an appropriate regional control is introduced. Further analysis reveals a negative rural production effect that withstands this control and sets the stage for a competitive test. The counter hypothesis rejects production organization of any size as causal, proposing instead that two dimensions of provincial structure—urban differentiation and pluralism—interact with efficient production organization, seen as an ad hoc factor, to determine welfare levels. A partial test of this structural mediation model explains much of the variance of infant mortality (the criterion of welfare). Scale has no effect.*

In 1946 two research reports were submitted to the Special Committee of the U.S. Senate to Study Problems of American Small Business. Both were destined to stimulate distinctive research traditions. One (Mills and Ulmer 1970) dealt with the impact of big business on community well-being while the other (Goldschmidt 1978a) examined the impact of big agriculture. Both the design and the theory of these studies were basically identical. Pairs of communities were matched on all but the hypothesized causal factor—the domination of large production organization—and the explanation of why such production organization would impact negatively turned on the intervening mechanism of class polarization. The study of big business impact emphasized the way business elites controlled communities and thereby reduced local autonomy, while the big agriculture study contended that a poorly paid rural proletariat undermined the local economy and weakened community participation.

The clarity of the hypotheses and the richly documented differences between the pairs of communities commanded assent. The approximation of a controlled experiment embodied in the research design was especially compelling, and the theoretical objections proposed in the half century since this research appeared were always made within the original materialist framework. In contrast, attempts to replicate these findings have not been so successful. Within a decade after the big business study, Fowler (1964) reported that the correlations across the thirty communities in his study, between big business impact and a range of indicators of community functioning, were positive, directly contradicting Mills and Ulmer. Inasmuch as Fowler used similar or identical measures to the earlier study, it was difficult to argue that the researchers did not address the same problem. Instead as Aiken and Mott (1970:83) put it, "the difference between Mills and Ulmer and Fowler have never been resolved; they still await a definitive examination" (but see Young and Lyson 1993).

Subsequent research on the Goldschmidt hypothesis was never so dramatically contradictory and has usually been reviewed as supportive. Nonetheless the literature includes enough reversals, failure to find any impact of large scale agriculture, and untested linkages to raise doubts (Lobao 1990; Swanson 1989). Given the clarity of theory, the strong methodology, and the definite findings of the original research, the failure after fifty years to accumulate overwhelming evidence in favor of these hypotheses is unsettling. The present study claims that what is needed is nothing less than a completely different way of looking at the relationship between production organization and the wellbeing of communities.

Before introducing the alternative formulation, it is important to understand exactly what Goldschmidt (1978a:415) was arguing: "The scale of operations inevitably skewed the occupational structure so that the majority of the population could only subsist by working as wage labor for others. . . . [This occupational structure] has had a series of direct effects upon the social conditions in the community." This three-step causal sequence may involve any or all of three mechanisms: lack of money to spend or, in the case of the absentee owners, spending it elsewhere; transient residence of the workers and/or big-city orientation of the owners; and lack of leadership from both classes.

The Goldschmidt hypothesis combines variables that occur in all parts of the world, and they can be measured in standard ways, so there is no reason in principle why it should not hold generally. Goldschmidt himself contributed to the generalization of his hypothesis with a study of the forty-eight mainland states (Goldschmidt 1978b). These variables are certainly operating in Chile, the locus of the present test. In the period under study (1975-1990), Chile had already experienced a partial land reform, breaking the power of the hacienda system. Although there are still many large farms in Chile, some may exceed the legal limit of eighty basic irrigated hectares (or about 500 mixed hectares). These and the farms of 100+ hectares employ hired labor for agricultural work.

This research has an additional aim, which is to introduce a non-materialist explanation of welfare that turns on structural mediation. This hypothesis holds that strong social structure, in the form of dimensions of social problem-solving capacity, combines with production organization to determine welfare levels. The scale of production organization is important only insofar as it affects the capacity of agriculture to produce profit and wages. Whether this economic impact increases or decreases the average welfare of the people in the community depends on the strength of social structure. If it is strong, the welfare effect of successful production organization will be enhanced, while deleterious impacts will be moderated or eliminated. If social structure is weak, permanently or temporarily, then production organization will have the negative impacts on welfare that Goldschmidt found. Even socially concerned owners can undermine average welfare if their organization is not regulated, buffered, and sometimes supported by the community.

The two dimensions of structure invoked in this research are, first, structural differentiation which, following long sociological usage, may be defined as the diversity of specialized organization, especially occupations. The second dimension is pluralism, the reciprocal communication and contestation among political actors, especially between the government and various sub-groups. These dimensions have a common rationale as institutionalized social problem-solving capacity. They are the "software" of society. When a community comes to define some cluster of events, from economic decline to toxic waste disposal, as a community problem, its problem-solving capacity is activated. The first line of defense consists of all the specialists who usually reside in the central city. Their various technical, legal, and negotiating skills are brought to bear, usually in the form of politically organized coalitions. If specialist knowledge proves to be inadequate, then pluralism comes into play, the issues become "political," and secondary and minority factions join the debate, usually with alternate proposals.

Unit of Analysis

Chile has fifty-one provinces, but only thirty-three are listed in the 1989 Census of Agriculture (*Instituto Nacional de Estadísticas* 1989-1990) as having significant agriculture. The 1975 Census of Agriculture (*Instituto*

Nacional de Estadisticas 1975-1976), which contains the information on size and labor force, lists only thirty-one provinces, so the two recently-formed provinces that appear in the 1989 census were reintegrated with the provinces from which they were formed.

Of the thirty-one provinces, sixteen (from Petorca, northeast of Santiago, to Linares, about 300 kilometers south of the capital) are classified as central. They correspond to Chile's Central Valley, which is both the urban and the agro-industrial core of the country. A wide range of temperate vegetables are grown, as well as grapes for domestic and export wine. This is also the region of the old haciendas, although now, after land reform, they have become commercial farms. In the South (but still in the agricultural provinces) are ten provinces (Nuble to Chiloe) with mostly large farms dedicated to cattle and wheat, while the five northern agricultural provinces (Copiapo to Choapa) have moved toward export agriculture, especially fruit, only in the last two decades.

The provincial unit of analysis raises the question of the locus of causality. The Goldschmidt hypothesis claims that causation begins in farm structure as it is aggregated up to dominance at the community level. So the question is how high to aggregate, and here practice is varied. In his later paper, Goldschmidt (1978b) used 48 U.S. states as units of aggregation, in sharp contrast to the original study that compared two towns with populations of 6,236 and 7,404. The community unit poses the question of how to count "surrounding farms," because many may be absentee-owned and may lie many miles from the community. Presumably, geographic proximity is fundamental because it determines the availability of a local worker population.

As soon as one departs from the small community unit, the presence of the nonfarm population and nonagricultural social structure complicates the analysis. Harris and Gilbert (1982) solved this problem in their study of U.S. states by confining all the variables to the rural sector and separating farm income from total rural income. Employing a different strategy, Lobao (1990) used countywide welfare criteria, but was able to focus on the impact of farm size by introducing nonagricultural variables as controls. This research will follow Lobao's lead.

Welfare Criteria

The official statistics in Chile do not contain measures of income or an estimate of an official poverty line, so these important criteria of development are unavailable for this study. Instead, infant mortality estimates from 1979 to 1988 were obtained (*Instituto Nacional de Estadisticas* (1986-1988). The three-year average for infant mortality over the years 1986 to 1988 was 22.2 (range: 15.1-31.6; SD: 4.4), a remarkable decline from 43.6 (range: 22.6-65.8; SD 11.6) in 1979-1980.

Infant mortality is one of several physical quality-of-life indicators that have moved to prominence as indicators of development in the last decade. Along with life expectancy, mortality, and measures of health status, infant mortality has become an expected supplement to the more conventional average income. It has two major advantages over average income, because it is a "final good" and it is not subject to large concentration bias. Unlike income, it cannot be hoarded by the rich. Consequently, changes in this criterion tend to reflect benefits to the poor. A further technical advantage is that births and infant deaths usually occur within the boundaries of the provincial unit of analysis. In contrast, the remittance of wages to home provinces can introduce a bias in the analysis of income.

Structural Dimensions and Intervening Variables

Along with the production indicators, the Chilean data includes the correlations for the two structural measures. The first is the percentage of the provincial population living in urban places in 1982 (*Instituto Nacional de Estadisticas* 1982). The mean is 63.7 (SD 16.8) with a wide range of 36.7 to 97.4. This proportion is limited to the inhabitants of cities and towns and is, therefore, more restrictive (and more precise) than the official census definition. This index is interpreted as specialization, because urbanized regions tend to have a greater diversity of occupations.

The index of pluralism is the percentage of the population who voted in the 1989 presidential election (mean 55%; SD 2.6; range 49-62). Total population was used as a base. The vote for 1989 was used instead of that for 1970 (Chile had no elections between these dates) because it is closer to the year of the infant mortality measure and it reflects the political processes of the post-coup 1980s. Also, the number of provinces doubled between the two dates, undermining comparability.

The percent voting is used as an index of pluralism because voting reflects both the participation and contestation dimensions that Dahl (1971) identified. Voting in Chile is contingent upon registration, and the categories of people who register depend on the scope of suffrage as defined by law. So voting constitutes an institutionalized form of communication with the government. In addition, pluralism implies contestation between parties and, indirectly, population segments. Percent voting correlates 0.49 with the percent of subsistence farms and negatively with the larger size categories.

Regional Variation

Both the Office of Technology Assessment (Swanson 1989) researchers and Lobao (1990) examined the scale hypothesis within the major regions of the United States, and both found variation by region. What is the point of these regional breakdowns? Lobao (1990) said they are not adequate proxies for agroclimatic factors or type of manufacturing. These should be measured separately. Nor are they adequate for historical interpretations that are sometimes made. Nonetheless, these regional contrasts can be illuminating. Lobao (1990:214) gave the following analysis: ". . . the sociopolitical context mediates the effects of industrialized farming and is particularly evident in the regional analyses. . . . In the Midwest . . . greater state regulation of corporate farming and a tradition of protection of family farming . . . may make industrialized farming more redistributive of benefits while the coercive agrarian and labor history of the South offers greater leeway for exploitation." Similarly, Skees and Swanson (1989) gave reasons for believing that context can blunt the negative impact of industrialized farming in southern U.S. countries. These explanations are suggestive, but Lobao's objection still holds: such hypothesized processes must be specified and tested separately. By this criterion, the demonstration by Gilles and Dalecki (1988) of a strong regional impact of the Great Plains versus the Corn Belt is the beginning, not the end, of research.

Farm Size and Infant Mortality

The initial statistical models (not shown) display the relationship of the proportion of large farms to infant mortality, controlling on urbanization. The large-farm category has a negative impact (i.e., a significant positive correlation with infant mortality), as anticipated by the Goldschmidt hypothesis. But contrary to the hypothesis, the medium and small categories also have negative impacts. The proportion of subsistence farms has a strong positive health impact, contrary to general expectation.

The large farm correlation is suspect because such farms are more frequent in the cattle/wheat provinces in the Chilean South, and it is unlikely that they are associated with a rural proletariat of the type Goldschmidt hypothesized. Thus, it is no surprise to see in another model that a control in the form of a dummy variable of southern location dissolves the initial relationship with large farms. Controlling on regional location is useful but never decisive. What is it about a particular region that accounts for the high infant mortality rates? Remnants of the Aracaunian Indians are concentrated in two of these provinces (Cautin and Malleco), and their infant mortality rate is high. But the southern region has a negative impact, even when these are controlled. A second factor is isolation. Only 58 percent of the southern provinces are urbanized as compared with 67 percent for the other agricultural provinces; it is likely also that rural dwellings are scattered around the edges of the large farms, in contrast to the small but nonurban clusters farther north.

In a further attempt to answer this question, another test added the percentages of farms with 20 to 99 hectares and temporary workers to urbanization and location in the South. Inasmuch as this medium farm category is associated with high infant mortality, the concentration of these farms in the South would explain its negative impact. Surprisingly, the effect of percent of temporary workers was in the opposite direction from that claimed by the Goldschmidt hypothesis. So now there are two questions: Why does temporary hired labor help to explain what goes on in the South, and why is it related to *low* infant mortality?

Answering the second question leads to the answer to the first. Temporary labor in the non-South (the Central Valley, especially) is a reliable source of income, because traditional crops grown there require a great deal of labor, and the work force is integrated into the whole system. In contrast, the dairy, cattle, and mechanized wheat farms in the South use less hired labor. The proportion of the labor force doing seasonal work is 14 percent as opposed to 25 percent in the non-South. But the key to this differential integration is the proportion of subsistence farms, which is somewhat less than 6 percent in the South and 31 percent in the other provinces. It appears that the South lacks a subsistence anchor point for its seasonal labor. The landless workers are simply left on their own.

None of these three processes corresponds to Goldschmidt's hypothesis of scale-generated inequality, so controlling on region is a legitimate delimitation of the sample. These processes can be interpreted in structural terms. The Indian populations lack autonomy and are disadvantaged in their dealings with government. Their scattered settlements lack service centers, an aspect of urbanization not well measured by the standard index. Finally, the unexpected finding that high proportions of temporary workers in the farm labor force are associated with low infant mortality illustrates a fundamental principle of structuralism, which is that "it depends." In the Central Valley the overall integration of the region works to integrate workers like these into the wider social fabric.

The Negative Impact of Export Expansion

From the perspective of a competitive test of the two explanations, the finding that once location in the South is controlled, large farms do not have a negative welfare impact while the medium-sized farms do is not an ideal outcome. Analysis then turned to identifying some other negative production effect. It is a fact of common observation that rapid social change frequently causes personal and family disruptions. Consequently, it is reasonable to expect to see these symptoms of change in Chile in those areas where export agriculture has expanded most rapidly. This expansion can be measured by calculating the ratio of land dedicated to export agriculture to that used for traditional crops. Inasmuch as export agriculture is mostly new since 1975, a high ratio should reflect expansion over the five-year period. If vegetables and fruits are considered export crops, in contrast to the mostly traditional vineyards and cereals, then the mean ratio of these two categories of agricultural land is 0.32 and 1.2 in 1975 and 1989, respectively. While measurement error in comparing figures from two different agricultural censuses is always a threat, the 1989 ratio (range 0-5.9; SD 1.4) seems to reflect the export expansion that is readily observed.

Model 1 in Table 1 tests this hypothesis. As before, the equation begins with urbanization and includes the South as a necessary control. In addition to the export ratio, the equation includes a necessary control on the area dedicated to export fruits and vegetables (mean 11.7; range 1-30.7; SD 9.0). The result in Model 1 is suggestive but not decisive, because the two export variables fall just short of significance. Model 2 adds the proportion of temporary farm workers, which reduces the impact of region while allowing the export ratio to show statistical significance. Thus, it appears that export expansion has a strong negative impact, correlating with high infant mortality when other variables are controlled.

The export expansion dislocation is not affected by processes in the South, nor is it controlled out by the degree of urbanization, which is what structural theory would anticipate. A major expansion of the economy such as this is equivalent to saying that whatever social structure may be in place will probably prove inadequate to the task, at least initially.

Table 1 Regression analysis of infant mortality in Chile on export and structural variables (N = 31)

Variables	1	2
Percent of population in urban areas	.041	-.044*
Percent agricultural land dedicated to fruits and vegetables	-0.35	-0.25
Ratio of land in export crops to land in traditional crops	0.40	0.40*
South	0.51*	0.41*
Percent who voted in 1989 presidential election		
Percent of agricultural labor force that is temporary		-0.31*
Adjusted R^2	0.54	0.60

*=Statistically significant at ≤ 0.05.

Is it possible that Goldschmidt mistook the temporary disruptive effects of California's expanding agriculture for the long-term impact of class polarization? Some of his facts are suggestive (Goldschmidt 1978a:325): "Both communities have a relatively large number of newcomers, but this group is far more numerous in Arvin than in Dinuba. Over half the Arvin residents came there in 1940 or later, while only about a fourth came to Dinuba during the same period." In the paragraph that precedes this one, Goldschmidt describes the newcomers to Arvin, most of whom arrived from the states of Oklahoma, Texas, and Arkansas. Another 12 percent of the family heads were foreign born, mostly in Mexico. In contrast, the hired labor in Dinuba migrated from Oklahoma, Texas, Missouri, and Kansas, and the foreign-born came from Canada, Armenia, and Russia. A lesser proportion came from Mexico. Summing up, Goldschmidt (1978a:415) states: "The large need for labor, and the period of major growth resulted in the aggregation of a large proportion of destitute white migrant labor with poor social and economic background. There is evidence that the quality of persons attracted by the kinds and conditions of work opportunities is somewhat poorer than was attracted to the situation in Dinuba".

It is true that in its visits to the two California towns, the Small Farm Viability Project (1977) found that Arvin had not improved much, a fact which contradicts the rapid expansion hypothesis. Also, Goldschmidt argued that such continuing labor turnover was due to the occupational structure, in line with this hypothesis. But it is easy to see that community-run facilities, as exist in Chile, could stabilize even such a labor force.

Conclusion and Discussion

The two purposes of this research were, first, to devise a fair test of the Goldschmidt hypothesis in the Chilean context and, second, to show that the empirical basis of the structural mediation hypothesis justifies its consideration as an alternative explanation.

Despite the foreign site, there is no reason to believe that scale and rural stratification could not be associated with different levels of welfare. Indeed, given the legacy of the hacienda system in Chile, the presumption was that the Goldschmidt hypothesis would be strongly supported. The first test showed, in fact, that the proportion of large-sized farms in a province was associated with lower quality of life, that is, high levels of infant mortality. But a control on the ten southern provinces, which were involved in non-Goldschmidt agricultural processes, undermined the initial relationship. Then, analysis turned to finding some other production-related process that had a demonstrable negative impact on quality of life. It appears that the expansion of export agriculture, as measured by the ratio of export hectares to that dedicated to domestic crops, has such a negative health impact, impervious to all controls.

Upon closer scrutiny, however, the export expansion effect corresponded to the Goldschmidt hypothesis only if it proved to be a long-term effect. Meanwhile, it could be interpreted in structural terms. Another result that went against the Goldschmidt hypothesis was the unexpected positive impact (low infant mortality) of the proportion of the agricultural labor force classified as temporary. This finding contradicts almost any kind of class-based explanation. Assuming the result would hold if the data pertained to the actual farmers rather than to provincial aggregates, the structural mediation approach argued that the welfare of farm workers depends on the overall rural structure, which in this case was benign.

Finally, the analysis (not shown) moved to a test of the two structural dimensions. Urbanization and voting made independent benign contributions even when the negative impacts of the southern region and the export expansion areas were included. Although it was not possible to demonstrate the interaction effect that the structural mediation hypothesis calls for, a control on health care, while making an independent contribution to lower infant mortality, did not affect the statistical significance of the other variables.

It must be apparent, despite the formal language of research reports, that this data set was full of surprises. It is quite possible that Chile is a special case. As far as they go, these findings support the structural mediation alternative to the Goldschmidt hypothesis. The test is admittedly incomplete, and with only thirty-one cases even patterns of statistically significant numbers that correspond to theory cannot be considered decisive. Still, having a structural alternative is important because the two positions are generic to sociology. The general materialist proposition pervades most of development theory. In opposition, sociological structuralism argues that production variables can never be reliable because they involve environmental transactions, and these are constantly changing.

Apart from intellectual competition, there is a practical reason for following up the mediation hypothesis. It implies a positive role for social structure. Unlike the "big agriculture" impact hypothesis, which offers only the alternative of opposing it or getting out of the way, structural mediation suggests the possibility of turning the impact of production organization to advantage. While it is true that urban specialization and political pluralism are not the kinds of things that extension workers can introduce to communities, we can at least understand how such problem-solving capacity can be brought to bear.

There is one last question. Why, then, did Goldschmidt get the results that he did? The structural answer is that social organization in Arvin was weak relative to the aggressive expansionism of its associated production organization. There is plenty of evidence for such a conclusion, because weak social structure was Goldschmidt's dependent variable. But the structural mediation hypothesis is not simply a claim for the reverse direction of causality, because production organization is one of two types of independent variables (along with structure) in the mediation formula, predicting a more refined measure of welfare (infant mortality rate). As such, it explicitly allows for the negative impacts that Goldschmidt observed. It also takes account of another aspect of the Goldschmidt hypothesis, the power of large land owners. In structural terms, such dominance is better interpreted as low pluralism, which can appear regardless of the scale of agriculture.

BRANCH PLANTS AND POVERTY IN THE AMERICAN SOUTH

Abstract: *An alternative to the widely accepted hypothesis that "big business" has a negative impact on community welfare is tested with data from 445 nonmetropolitan counties in the American South. We argue that the appropriate counter-hypothesis is not that branch plants have a positive or negative impact on community welfare, because that and similar formulations simply perpetuate the nonsociological approach of the early hypotheses. An interaction formulation that sees community structure as mediating the impact of branch plants better explains differentials in three criteria of welfare—per capita income, percent below the poverty line, and infant mortality. This explanation predicts higher welfare when pluralism and urbanization are high and branch plants are numerous. Welfare is lower when one or all of these is low. Tests using discriminant analysis support the interaction hypothesis while providing little evidence for either the direct positive or negative impact hypotheses.*

The Lynds' study of Middletown (1929) probably deserves the credit for initiating the sociological study of industrial domination, but the Mills and Ulmer (1946/1970) study of three matched pairs of communities in the American Midwest contributed both a testable and tested formulation. These authors began their study with the populist claim that "big business tends to depress while small business tends to raise the level of civic welfare" (1946/1970:124). The first part of their report stresses the characteristics of the industry, specifically the degree of concentration and the consequent greater vulnerability of big business to instability in employment and wages. Associated with these negative consequences were lower levels of retail trade and middle-class strength. As a consequence of such vulnerability, what are now called "social indicators" are uniformly lower. Paralleling the vulnerability theme, Mills and Ulmer identify a mechanism of control based on the overt threat to move the factory. They go on to argue that "the influence of corporation men is often exerted surreptitiously, behind the concealing façade of local puppets and official figureheads" (1946/1970:146). In this way, big business exerts negative pressure via a monolithic power structure.

About a decade later, Irving Fowler (1964) reported the results of his doctoral research, a test of the Mills and Ulmer propositions on thirty New York state industrial cities. In direct opposition to the earlier study, Fowler found that "big business communities," as defined by employment concentration and absentee ownership, had higher levels of welfare than the small business cities. He further concluded that the least pluralistic power structures (low industrial unionism, small "old" middle class, low political "liberalism," etc.) were associated with higher levels of welfare. Last, he found that heavier durable goods industries were located in higher welfare places (1964:162).

Aiken and Mott (1970:83) suggest that the Eastern vs. Midwestern regional locations may account for the differences between the two studies, but of course that simply deepens the puzzle. Fowler homes in on the postulated monolithic power structure as decisive. He denies its reality, arguing that Mills and Ulmer "abstracted from their data only that which permitted the construction of a malevolent picture" (1970:160). He concedes that periodic abuse of power by modern industries occurs, but argues that it has provoked defensive-protective reactions on the part of buyers and sellers. More generally, he claims that the exercise of industrial power in Western democracies has been sharply delimited.

Both Aiken and Mott's hypothesis of regional differences and Fowler's discussion of countervailing power suggest an interaction formulation: that the impact of industrial organization on welfare levels is mediated by community structure. The problem, of course, is to specify which variables of organization are crucial, but here we can draw on classical dimensions: levels of urban specialization and political pluralism. They suggest the following general formulation: *Welfare levels are a function of the interaction of branch plant impact and the level of pluralism and of urban differentiation.* Both business and strong social organization are necessary for high levels of welfare. If one is missing, or if both are weak, then welfare levels will be low. It follows that researchers must examine community organization in combination with business differences. In this way we propose to meet the challenge of Aiken and Mott's summary statement: "The differences between Mills and Ulmer and Fowler have never been resolved; they still await a definitive examination" (1970:83).

Why research a question that is almost fifty years old? If it is a good question, then age should not make a difference, and in this case we know that this research helped launch a long and important series of "community power" studies. With hindsight it is also clear that this paradigm represented one strand of an emerging neo-Marxism. From this perspective, Mills' hypothesis translates as follows: Capitalistic production leads to class polarization, which undermines community institutions and contributes to the immiseration of the workers. "Community power" in this framework is Marx's "executive committee" writ small, and behind the populist phrase "big business" is a heavy materialist assumption.

An additional reason for this research is purely intellectual: It is not often in sociology that two well-designated studies do not talk past each other yet come to exactly opposite conclusions. The usual situation is either that a second research fails to confirm the initial research or the replication is only partial. What we have here is a head-on collision, the kind that often forces radical conceptual reformulations.

There are also practical implications. Branch plants are probably the modal type of industrial organization in the world today. They are spreading in less developed countries while American communities fight to attract or hold such plants. If it is true, as Mills and Ulmer claim, that large branch plants undermine the communities in which they locate, then a kind of social disease is spreading around the world that demands sociological analysis.

Structural Interactions and Welfare

The fundamental hypothesis of the big business impact explanation can be expressed simply as $w = (o)$, where w is some measure of individual or family welfare and o is a whole range of external economic organizations. For the purposes of this research, "o" will refer to large, outside-owned industry, which is the core feature of Mills and Ulmer's "big business." The formula is essentially the same for the detractors and supporters of industry; only the sign changes. It applies also to a third hypothesis, which is that locally owned firms contribute to improved welfare.

In opposition to this simplistic formula, which ignores local social structure, we propose that $w = (o \times s)$, where s is community structure. Community structure is specified by two widely accepted dimensions—level of urban specialization and political pluralism—which we argue reflect fundamental dimensions of social problem-solving capacity. The importance of specialization, structural differentiation, or the division of labor goes back at least to Durkheim, and it is central to American "human ecology" studies. Key sources are Schnore (1958), Bogue (1961), and Clemente and Sturgis (1972). The literature on pluralism and its cognates (competitiveness, polyarchy) is usually anchored in Tocqueville's writings, with statements by Key (1951), Dahl (1971), and Bollen (1980). Dahl's major theme is that polyarchy embodies two dimensions: contestation and participation (suffrage). When voting statistics are available and comparable, as they are in the United States, then it is reasonable to treat these as a general measure for competitiveness and participation.

How do these dimensions mediate the environment? It is necessary, first, to specify the two types of problems posed by the branch plants: they pressure communities to offer subsidies to attract the plants, and the pressure to maintain a social, political, and economic climate that insures the maximum profitability of the plant. Among other things, plants want tax remission or reduction, subsidized construction and installation and lower costs, especially for labor. Once in operation, they try to externalize as many of their costs as possible: waste disposal, housing, education, and other needs of the employees. They look for weak unions, so that losses can be spread to workers in the form of layoffs.

These disadvantages to the locality are balanced against obvious advantages, such as wages and their spread effects to the retail sector, subcontracts with local suppliers, and even philanthropic contributions by the outside owners. These perceptions of advantage and disadvantage are based on constant monitoring of the environment. Threats and opportunities are continuously shifting in response to changes in products and markets. Indeed, the very definition of what is an advantage or disadvantage is often at issue.

Specialization and pluralism enable counties to deal with the branch plant environment by a process of group-level problem management, which includes problem definition and problem solving. The role of specialization in this process is elaborated in Aiken and Alford's (1970) analysis of urban renewal in American cities. For these authors, the size of cities is a proxy for structural differentiation. The larger the city, the greater the number of organizations devoted to relevant kinds of decision areas: housing agencies, city engineering departments, etc. Similarly, large cities are more likely to have government and business organizations prepared to recruit and accommodate branch plants. For any given problem, subsets of local organizations are likely to form coalitions in order to marshal the resources necessary to address the issue at hand. Most community problems, after all, are recurring or present in other places, so the availability of expert "puzzle solvers" is the major consideration.

If the problems are beyond the capacities of structural differentiation, pluralism intensifies. By permitting and encouraging minority opinion, communities allow unconventional ideas to rise to the surface of political debate. Pluralism also helps build a consensus around a particular solution. V. O. Key's (1951:208 ff.) analysis of how pluralism tends to benefit the poor in southern states throws light on these processes. Although the case is made indirectly, Key argues the beneficial effects of competition for votes in a two-party environment. A precondition for such competition is institutionalized expression of diverse interests, and the second is broad-based suffrage. Given these, there is a long-term bias in favor of the interests of disadvantaged groups who, by virtue of numbers, hold electoral power.

There is no guarantee, of course, that the correct policy will be selected or that it will continue to be appropriate over time. But the signal system of the political marketplace will then be reactivated and alternative solutions will be reviewed. Since the environment never rests, neither can the community's problem-solving organization. Very likely other dimensions of problem-solving capacity can be formulated. Social movements, for example, may be more likely to appear when the resolution of a problem requires a major reorganization of the community. Likewise, articulation with superordinate system levels may be necessary for resolving other types of problems. But specialization and pluralism are certainly two fundamental dimensions in this respect and constitute an important part of the meaning of "strong organization."

The structural mediation hypothesis unites the general problem-solving capacity of communities with the technical organization involved in environmental transactions. Essentially, it states that in addition to production, two kinds of general problem-solving organization are required for improving welfare. While not denying the importance of production organization, health and welfare bureaucracies, and even federal subsidies, it implies that all of these are inadequate without a strong structural matrix. The interaction hypothesis should hold for all levels of industrial concentration, and for different types of industry (light versus heavy goods, etc.). We make this claim, even though it is not tested, to highlight the generality of our approach and because we believe that the arguments for refinements—like concentration of production and type of enterprise—lead to ambiguous conclusions. Granted that one or a few dominant industries could impact negatively on the community, the opposite positive effect could also occur if management happened to be benign. At the other end of the continuum, many branch plants in a community could exacerbate any negative impacts or, because of competition among the factories, reduce them. Likewise, the positive or negative impact of type of industry is not clear. Advocates of the hypothesis that "heavy" industry will have a negative impact give no reason. There seems to be an implicit assumption that the managers of light industry are "nicer," but, of course, they could also be more devious. In any event, the mediation hypothesis implies that whatever the presumed positive or negative impacts, the final outcome depends on the level of urban specialization and pluralism of the impacted communities. How could it be otherwise? Industry is rarely all-powerful and communities almost always have organizational resources. The idea that external organizations have a direct impact ignores that many communities are themselves strong organizations, capable of strong countermeasures.

Summary and Discussion

This research has identified four hypotheses relevant to the impact of branch plants on family and individual welfare. The first is the Mills and Ulmer claim that branch plants have negative impacts. The second asserts the opposite, positive, relationship. A third hypothesis that is embedded in the Mills and Ulmer text holds that locally owned firms should have positive impacts in contrast to the negative or unspecified impacts of outside-owned firms. The fourth proposition, which is supported by this research, rejects all of these, asserting instead that average welfare depends on the buffering capacity of local social structure with respect to industrial activity, whether external or locally owned. The Mills and Ulmer intervening variable is ignored because monolithic power is simply a transmission mechanism, and does not fundamentally modify the impact of the branch plants. All four of these hypotheses are formulated, of course, net of background factors and, in the case of the interaction formulation, the direct effects of the various components. The results of a discriminant analysis (not shown) of three welfare criteria—

per capita income, percent below the poverty line, and infant mortality—supported the mediation hypothesis as follows:

1. The number of branch plants had a significant direct impact on only one of the three welfare criteria, infant mortality, in line with the Mills and Ulmer hypothesis.

2. The number of locally owned firms had only one effect, also on infant mortality, but it contradicted the hypothesis. Interaction effects with local firms were nonsignificant in all cases.

3. The first interaction term, the number of branch plants by percent urban, had no effect on infant mortality, but the relationships to per capita income and poverty were significant and in the predicted direction.

4. The second interaction term, branch plants by percent voting, showed a strong negative relationship, as hypothesized, with infant mortality, and weaker but significant positive links to income and poverty.

These results held in analyses that controlled for the criterion variable at an earlier point in time, as well as the direct impact of percent voting, percent urban, and two demographic control variables. Of the latter, percent black performed as expected: It was positively related to infant mortality and poverty and negatively to per capita income. Percent population change for the 1970 decade was negatively related to poverty and to income level.

We interpret these results as grounds for rejecting all three direct impact formulations and for accepting the interaction hypothesis. Since this conclusion is based on the use of an unconventional technique, it is well to review this methodology. We introduced discriminant analysis because it is, in fact, more appropriate than a lagged panel regression that requires the assumption of linear relationships between all the independent variables, including, in this case, the interaction terms and the criterion variables. Rejecting this assumption recognizes the possibility that the relationships are not linear, at least in some segments of the distribution. Therefore, trichotomizing the dependent variable as required by discriminant analysis is actually more accurate, despite the loss of information with respect to the continuous dependent variables. The generation of a second function, although not a strong one, further reduced the nonlinearity threat.

One can ask, as we did, whether the method itself could have produced these results. We think not, for the following reasons: First, the shift to discriminant analysis was made after exploratory analysis revealed the nonlinear patterns that discriminant analysis can handle better. Second, our results hold across three distinct criterion variables. And third, our results correspond to a complex and unconventional prediction. Although the role of structure in mediating the environment is fundamental to the sociological enterprise, tests of structure vs. production organization are noticeably absent in the literature.

Turning to the hypotheses themselves, we call attention to an implication that we believe will have substantive repercussions in other studies. What the interaction hypothesis does, we claim, is to call into question all theoretical perspectives that assert a direct causal role for external impacts on communities. The interaction formulation rejects the primary causal status of outside firms. Now they are copartners with the social organization of the community. Their potential for making a profit and contributing to the material welfare of the community is still crucial, but now the social organization of the impacted social system is central.

The Mills and Ulmer research dangles one last question: How would the interaction hypothesis explain the contradictory results of Mills and Ulmer and Fowler? In general, it would expect Fowler's communities to have stronger social organization than those of Mills and Ulmer. Higher levels of urbanization and voting in the upstate New York communities, in combination with the branch plants, would generate higher welfare levels. The branch plants in the Mills and Ulmer study should be located in communities with lower levels of urbanization and voting.

REGIONAL STRUCTURE IN SUB-SAHARAN AFRICA

Abstract: *The urban hierarchies of 280 subnational regions of sub-Saharan Africa are shown to be systematically related to ecological and economic indicators all across Africa, despite that continent's cultural and ecological diversity. Using data from detailed maps of Africa, it appears that urban hierarchy, indexed by the number of cities with a population of 20,000 or more, correlates with the number of towns, population of the largest place, population of the region, density, number of industries (both agricultural and general), and even ecological features like lakes, forests, and dams. Additionally, and surprisingly, the number of different agricultural export crops in the region and the number of different minerals that are exploited correlate with the number of cities.*

Social research on contemporary Africa is polarized between studies that look at the national units from the "top" down and those, like anthropological and farming systems studies, that report the detail of micro situations. Limitations on resources for research and the interests of donor organizations and research institutes, mainly in industrialized countries, probably determine the distribution. The national unit, particularly government and economic structure, is of primary interest to organizations like the World Bank, the UN and the state departments of Western countries. The dynamics of local communities or farming systems are of interest to university-based scholars and development agencies. Between these two levels lies a relatively unexamined range of phenomena that are indicated by the phrase "subnational regional structure." These units, especially provinces and districts, are usually studied by national professionals, and such research frequently depends on the availability of census information more detailed than the standard population censuses; accordingly, it is usually the last to be undertaken. When it is, it is almost invariably focused on particular countries.

The research reported here contributes to research on subnational units. Yet instead of census data or other official statistics, it makes use of indices derived from detailed maps of African countries. It argues the utility of the first order administrative units, and demonstrates the capacity of the urban hierarchies of these regions to organize many important features of these units. The patterns found in the course of this research are not as detailed as those derived from "cross-state" studies in developing countries, but they hold all across Africa and vary systematically with the major ecological zones of that continent.

This research is based on two fundamental operational assumptions. The first is that administrative units are appropriate "regions" in Africa. As compared to units based on physical ecology or units constructed from the spread of metropolitan urban influence, administrative units are obviously easier to identify. For the most part, their boundaries are readily available on the maps. The only problem that this study encountered was the lack of province-sized units in some countries. In those cases, as discussed below, districts were grouped following quasi-administrative regional boundaries.

The second and, perhaps, the most important reason for using administrative units is that their boundaries channel the influence of the national government. Although many African governments are weak, they still appoint governors, control the country militarily, and extract taxes. Capital projects, if they exist, are located in particular regions, and decisions pertaining to them are almost always political. Even in Africa, where the physical ecology is a major force, the most important feature of a region's "environment" is the national government. The frequent claims that administrative boundaries are arbitrary usually refer to the national boundaries which were, in fact, drawn up in European capitals. But subnational boundaries were probably more sensitive to the human populations in Africa.

Apart from their intrinsic interest, administrative units can always be compared in later research to units based on the physical ecology or urban hinterlands. Meanwhile, a demonstration of statistical patterns using these units provides preliminary evidence of the "reality" of subnational regions. If their attributes did not interact to some degree, it is difficult to see how correlations could be found. On the same argument, to jump ahead of the story, the demonstration of such correlations is evidence that measurement error, which is always present in the identification of boundaries, was not so great as to obscure the basic patterns. The second assumption of this study is that a simple count of cities (with population over 20,000) is an adequate index of the degree of urban hierarchy in these regions. Here the question is whether a count of cities corresponds to accepted definitions of hierarchy and to widely used conventions for measuring such hierarchy. O'Conner's (1983:240) definition provides a good starting point. The urban hierarchy, he says, involves "many centers which depend on fewer large centers for more specialized functions. At all levels, of course, such hierarchical spatial structures are reflecting hierarchical power structures." The basic elements, then, are: (a) centers stratified on the basis of similarity of function, (b) pyramidal shape, with more "lower" than higher centers, and (c) asymmetrical relations, with the higher centers influencing the lower. O'Conner mentions that the higher centers are often administrative, and suggests that the direction of influence is from the capital city to provincial headquarters and down to the district. Writers working out of the central-place tradition (Marshall 1969) tend to emphasize commercial functions, and these are less obviously asymmetrical. At the other extreme, O'Conner mentions "dualistic hierarchies," where a European urban system is superimposed on and dominates the indigenous system.

Against this conceptual background, a simple count of cities, as used here, has the advantage that the urban unit is front and center, but it has the disadvantage that the influence hierarchy is not measured. If the proper analogy with urban hierarchies is the chain of command among military officers, then the index of urban hierarchy used here is like knowing the number of officers in a division, but not knowing which are the generals, the colonels, etc. On the other hand, the number of cities in African regions tends to be few, so the administrative status of the provincial capitals looms large. So if a province has no cities with a population of 20,000 or more, it is clear that the provincial capital must be a minor place. If a province has only one city with a population of 20,000 or more, it clearly dominates the hierarchy. If there are two or more such cities, the direction of influence is unclear, but it is still reasonable to suppose that the provincial capital dominates the commercial centers, even if these are the same size or larger. If that is not the case, then multi-city provinces may be thought of as containing an administrative and a commercial hierarchy.

Therefore, the two proposed entry points to the study of subnational regions in Africa can be justified. Administrative units reflect an important organizational reality, and the number of cities in such provinces is a reasonable index of the well-known tendency of cities to structure their hinterlands. What remains, then, is an empirical test of these presuppositions. This research seeks to demonstrate that: (a) subnational regional urban hierarchies can be measured in the 280 subnational regions of 40 sub-Saharan African countries, (b) these hierarchies organize or are at least congruent with fundamental features of the regional economies, and (c) the criterion of urban hierarchy levels used here, the number of places larger than 20,000 can be predicted on the basis of ecological and economic features of the regions.

Characteristics of Subnational Regions in Africa

The principal source of data for this study is the detailed information contained in the maps of the *Cultural Atlas of Africa* (Murray, 1982). The boundaries of the units are the official administrative lines or, where these units were too small (Ivory Coast, Guinea, Uganda), the larger subnational areas that most countries recognize. In most cases, these have a certain legitimacy for the national government. The number of regions ranged from one to eighteen (Tanzania) in the forty sub-Saharan countries (dropping South Africa and the small islands). The mean was 7 regions. Seven countries (Burundi, Djibouti, Gambia, Guinea-Bissau, Lesotho, Rwanda and Swaziland) were treated as single units.

The *Cultural Atlas* gave no indication of the size of the urban centers, so that information was coded from the Rand McNally *Great Geographical Atlas* (1982), which distinguished two sizes of places above and below 20,000 people. These are here called "cities" and "towns." This dichotomy is the basis of the index of hierarchy levels shown in Table 1, which simply divides the 280 regions into those with no cities, one city only, and two or more cities.

As already mentioned, this research uses a simple count of cities in a region to index the complexities of the urban hierarchy: Cities are surrounded by dependent towns; they are connected by roads, trade, and political ties; and the larger places influence the smaller ones rather than the reverse. Although some direct evidence on these points is presented, the basic claim at this point is simply that the index "worked." The number of hierarchy levels is limited to three because of the paucity of regions with three or more cities, and because, probably, such multi-city areas reflect special circumstances, such as a large territory or a precolonial history of urbanization.

A trained coder, using a transparent overlay showing the subnational boundaries, counted the number of times a given crop, mineral, or some fact of infrastructure appeared in each subnational region, and this information was transferred to a computer file. Then the separate counts were combined according to empirical categories like "fiber crops" or "food grains." These composite scores constitute the variables that helped to interpret the character of urban hierarchies, as described below.

Certainly there are errors in this data set. The facts themselves are imprecise, and errors were doubtless made in the collection of these facts and in their location on the maps. Such errors may be compounded by subnational boundaries that do not coincide with the influence of urban hierarchies, as already discussed. To these frequently heard criticisms one can reply as follows: All data sets have errors, and insofar as they are unbiased they simply weaken the results. Second, the facts are adequate for the problem at hand and, indeed, are more likely to be accurate than relevant official statistics, if such were available. After all, the identification of sorghum or uranium mining for a certain part of the country is fairly straightforward. And third, the alternative of using information from maps is to sit on our hands, because comparable official statistics will probably never exist. Even if each of these forty countries had a detailed census of population and agriculture, the categories from one country to the next would not be comparable, and the dates for which the data were collected could not possibly coincide. By contrast, the information in this map-based data set pertains up to about 1980, and the information, which was assembled by a team of geographic specialists, is relatively uniform.

Some of the salient characteristics of African hierarchies are shown in Table 1. As the number of cities increases, so does the number of towns, evidence of pre-colonial urbanization; population density; the population of the region; and kilometers of rail. Some of these indicators are partially redundant with number of cities, but others, such as number of towns and population density, support the hierarchy assumption. Two variables, road mileage and national capitals (not shown), do not correlate well, probably because so many of the single city provinces are compact. If these "Washington, DCs" are deleted from the sample, the correlations are even stronger.

Table 1 Means of regional characteristics by number of cities (N=280)

N Regions	N Cities	N Towns	Pre-colonial urbanization	Population density (per km2)	Population region (000's)	Km rail
95	0	11	.11	12	448	66
117	1	11	.32	18	1057	111
68	2+	19	.38	22	2800	280

Considering the widely held opinion that significant generalizations about Africa are virtually impossible, the degree of order demonstrated in Table 1 is remarkable. The correlations extend even to the number of dams, lakes, and forests in the regions and their geographical location. Of course, it makes no sense to say that the urban hierarchy "organizes" these features of the physical ecology, but clearly such environments, mainly in the highlands, favored the appearance of large urban concentrations.

Other facts about the two components (towns and cities) of these hierarchies are that the mean number of cities for all 280 subnational regions is 1.1 while that for towns rounds off to 13. The minimum for both is zero, although there is only one region with no towns. There are 95 regions with *no* cities. The distributions of the two variables contrast sharply. That for cities meets our expectations with most of the regions classified as 0 or 1, after which the frequencies fall off rapidly, effectively terminating at 6, although there is one region with 7 cities and another with 11. That outlier is Western state, Nigeria. The extreme case for towns is Haut, Zaire, with a total of 96. Other regions had 79 towns, 58, and on down. In fact, 15 percent of these regions have 21 towns or more.

Table 2 shows the means of a number of economic indicators by level of hierarchy, along with the correlation coefficients. The number of general industries increases from a mean of .2 in regions with no cities to 2.6 in the single city provinces, and then to 4.2 for provinces with two or more cities. The basis for scoring regions on the "general industries" category is shown in the lower part of the table, where examples of the kinds of detail shown on the maps are given. For all 280 regions, the mean number of industries was 3.8, with a maximum of 19. That is, at least one region actually had 19 industries.

The agricultural industry count brings out another attribute of these scores, because it is apparent that the list contains many functional alternatives. If the region's ecology favored cassava, one might find cassava processing—otherwise cotton ginning, or some other agricultural industry could be present. That is also true of the food grain category, but it and fiber exports involve another consideration, which is that the number of areas shown on the map where a given commodity is grown was also counted. This procedure introduces a certain element of ambiguity in the count, but it seems more faithful to the African reality where the same crop may not be identical in its production organization if grown in another ecology. Note, however, that multiple locations were not counted for the two categories of mining. The detail on the maps did not permit an accurate count.

Table 2 Means of selected economic activities by number of cities (N = 280)

Level of Hierarchy	General Industries	Agricultural Industries	Food Grains	Fiber Exports	Traditional Mining	Strategic Mining	N
0	.2	.5	3.1	.5	.3	3	95
1	2.6	2.3	4.2	.8	.4	3	117
2+	4.2	3.5	3.9	1.4	.6	1.2	68
Correlation	.47	.43	.12	.26	.14	.21	

General industries=Aluminum metallurgy, asphalt, basic metallurgy, boat building, brewing (plus forty-eight others); Agricultural industries=Abattoir, banana processing, cassava processing, cotton ginning (plus twenty-five others); Food grains=Maize, millet, sorghum, rice, wheat, barley; Fiber exports = Cotton, kapok, cassava, rubber, sisal; Traditional mining=diamonds, gold, iron, platinum, and silver; Strategic mining=Cadmium, chrome, cobalt (plus twenty-one similar substances).

Coding note: Minerals were coded simply present or absent in a region. For agricultural commodities it was also possible to count the number of areas in which a crop was grown.

The correlation between number of general industries and urban hierarchy is .47. Inasmuch as almost all of these industries were located in the cities, and industry is implied by the definition of large centers, this correlation probably represents the ceiling for the levels of association in this study. The difference between .47 and a perfect correlation reflects measurement error or cross-cutting variables. Interestingly, the number of agricultural industries shows a strong correlation with urban hierarchy levels, indicating that such industries are concentrated in the city regions, much more than one might find in an industrial country. After that, however, the correlations drop, especially for food grains where the means suggest a curvilinear relationship.

Conclusion and Discussion

The comparison of subnational regions reported here reveals systematic regularities, both from the point of view of the correlates of urban hierarchy levels and the determinants of such levels. While these patterns are consistent with the claim that the urban hierarchy is a master organizing structure for regions, we cannot assert, on the basis of this evidence, that the urban hierarchy organizes political and cultural life because the correlates were economic. The analysis did show the strong conditioning influence of the physical ecology, especially the contrast between the coastal and hinterland zones in the coastal countries.

These patterns emerged despite the crude map-derived indices. While it is likely that the breakdown by ecological zone and the use of composite scores of alternative commodities in different parts of Africa improved the sensitivity of the analysis, urban hierarchy research can still be refined if and when the relevant statistics become available. In particular, the index for urban hierarchy levels must capture the asymmetrical relationships among higher and lower centers. Another source of error is the possibility that the administrative boundaries used in this study to define regions did violence to the "true" urban hierarchy, for instance, as defined by network criteria. Future work must explore alternative definitions of region. Meanwhile, administrative boundaries have the advantage of corresponding to national government policy units.

This research has only scratched the surface. Despite the role that urban hierarchies seem to play in organizing subnational regions in Africa and elsewhere, and despite the importance of the core principle of specialization in almost all theories of development, it is unreasonable to assume that specialized hierarchies are the only organizing structure, or even the strongest one, in all regions. Regional structure is more than urban hierarchy. In Latin America, the role of landed elites and the plantation form of production is well known. This form of class rigidity is perhaps an extreme, but hierarchy based on control of production and access to the market is universal. Likewise, ethnic organization can function like class. Minor ethnic groups are usually under the control of the larger dominant unit. A third principle, different from either functional specialization or class and ethnic rigidity, is solidarity, which takes the form of regional "nationalism" in most parts of the world. Mild forms of provincial pride and patriotism are well known in advanced industrial countries. The same phenomenon exists in Africa and frequently surfaces when the region is under threat. The economic and cultural vitality of southeastern Nigeria (Biafra) is well known, along with that of Eritrea in Ethiopia.

An adequate description of regional organization must identify and measure these fundamental principles of structure. They involve considerable theoretical underpinning, to be sure, but conceptualization is possible and such patterns can be measured. The fundamental assumption is that organizational capacities such as these are crucial to the regional development process and, when the regions of a nation are taken together, to national development.

SECTION 3
SOCIAL EPIDEMIOLOGY

Overview

Social epidemiology is the subfield of epidemiology that integrates behavioral risk factors like smoking, inactivity, and the like with the biomedical explanation of diseases and mortality. It also works with positive determinants such as education, and it is fair to say that the central problem for social epidemiology is the explanation of the strong correlation between education, income, and similar socioeconomic indicators, on the one hand, and measures of population health, on the other. My entry into this debate is the first article in this section, which reviews the many attempts to explain the SES-health correlation and then introduces a sociological explanation. It breaks with the biomedical explanation of disease and mortality by hypothesizing a direct causal link between population health and SES, interpreted as the superior problem-solving households.

The second paper in this group is a "storks and babies" analysis, one that shows that the claims for causality are spurious once a test variable—agrarian family organization, in the textbook illustration—is introduced. Here, however, the test variable is "industrializing region," which brings together an over-supply of doctors and many sick peasants who do the industrial work. The doctors are there because the demand for their services in the Tokyo metropolitan region has been met and they are looking for new opportunities. At the same time, and independently, the real causal process is occurring when rural people migrate to industrializing cities where the stress of adjustment takes a toll on their health. Spurious correlations like this are fairly common in the social sciences.

The same mistake is not so obvious when a measure of income inequality is correlated with a high death rate. That particular causal claim is rejected in the third paper, which demonstrates that the test variable "white status loss" across the US states is the true cause of poor health and social problems. Like the storks in the textbook example, the high Gini coefficient of income inequality is adventitious. The test variable is "location in the South," but of course the causal mechanism that operates in this region must be pin-pointed, as above. Coming up with the true causal explanation can be difficult, but making the assumption that causality is a group-level process and not the consequence of the aggregated individual characteristics usually brings success.

The final paper in this group makes the case for a "social problems public health," but the title ends with a question mark. Perhaps it should have ended with several question marks, because we are looking at the initial question of the validity of the theory, the needed measurements, monitoring, and the feasibility of a new branch of public health. The phrase "social problems" in this title refers to all the community-interpreted events that are threats to communities. Classifying such threats is a large task in itself. That leaves the radical proposal of a social ecology-based public health, one that will attempt to control the spread of social problems and, if possible, find ways to moderate the impact of the worst threats.

SOCIOECONOMIC STATUS AND HEALTH: THE PROBLEM OF EXPLANATION AND A SOCIOLOGICAL SOLUTION

Abstract: *The task of explaining why socioeconomic status (SES) and health are strongly correlated has grown beyond the special problem of the "gradient." It is now evident that the stepwise relationship of measures of health with years of schooling and similar indicators is only one of several features that must be explained. These include its association with a broad spectrum of diseases, the way SES predicts across the life course, and the widening gap between the health status of those with low and high SES. Even more significant than these is the persistence of the correlation, despite numerous controls for mediating variables such as medical access, chronic illnesses, and lifestyle indicators. The conclusion that the effect is direct and unmediated is increasingly probable, but a codification of the biomedical explanation of "wellness" reveals that the direct effect contradicts the model. An alternative "structural" explanation is outlined that resolves the contradiction, but at the price of rejecting the biomedical theory as an explanation of direct social effects like SES. The new theory leaves the biomedical explanation intact for the curative medicine and epidemics, but it points to a sociological rationale for public health programs oriented to enhancing positive health.*

It is only recently, according to Adler and Ostrove (1999), that researchers have become conscious of the need to find one or more "mechanisms" that link socioeconomic status to health. Previous research (circa 1970-1984) was content to "control SES out" to demonstrate that a proposed risk factor, say, lack of exercise, showed an independent effect. Now it is clear that the "SES effect" on health can no longer be ignored. It is strong, multifaceted, and persists despite controls on the many variables that the biomedical explanation embodies.

The Problem

Almost all discussions of the SES problem take "population health" rates as the object of explanation. Extrapolating the discussion in Evans *et al.* (1994), population health may be taken as an umbrella term for a cluster of generally accepted measures such as life expectancy, self-reported health status, clinical assessments, and functional ability. Consequently "health" is a consensus-based family of indicators. Rates of disease may qualify as population measures, but they differ from those listed in being (organic) site-specific.

Socioeconomic status is also a cluster of indicators of desirable individual and family attributes. They include income, wealth, material possessions, occupational prestige, and similar characteristics. The list also includes education, in the sense of years of schooling, and related cultural attributes, such as social participation, that are closely associated with it. The theoretical interpretation for these measures is still being debated (after more than a century). Therefore, the indicators will be handled empirically, which is how they are treated in the literature. Measures of income inequality are excluded from the discussion because they turn on a different principle.

Essentially, then, we are looking at the interrelationships of two clusters of social indicators. The challenge is to find an adequate explanation for the associations between them. Such an explanation should provide guidance for the choice and construction of indicators as well as the nature of the intervening "mechanisms." Indicators of the proposed mediators—medical access, lifestyle habits, physiology, and the like—must be shown to be correlated with SES, and also with a measure of health; and empirical tests should reduce the initial correlation to zero (or close to it). Given the problems of measurement, no single test is likely to be conclusive, but this essay contends that we already know enough to judge whether current efforts will ultimately be successful.

Four SES Effects

The best-known feature of the SES-health association is that it takes the shape of a "gradient" when displayed as a bar graph. The term gradient refers to a stepwise relationship of a higher level of health with each year of schooling or other SES measure. In other words, the correlation holds at all SES levels. (Haan et al. 1989; Elo and Preston 1996; Kaplan 2001; Kitagawa and Hauser 1973; Marmot et al. 1997; Syme and Berkman 1976; among others). It is not a problem of a threshold effect that separates the very poor from the rest of the distribution. According to the Dutton and Levine review (1989; also Syme 1996), the gradient holds for both sexes, all ages, and everywhere it has been studied; and the indicator of SES does not significantly change the result. (See Macken-bach et al., 2002 for the European findings.)

The data source for the example presented here is NHANES III, the National Health and Nutrition Examination Survey (1997), a well-known national survey that contains two global measures of health status, a self-rating, and a doctor's assessment. It also contains a broad range of social and physical variables of the type required for exploring the SES effect. (See Ferraro and Farmer 1999 and Burt et al. 1995, for technical description.)

Figure 1 shows the distinctive pattern, especially for the upper grades, where retrospective memory is probably better. For men, the percent reporting their health as "excellent" increased relative to the previous level for 14 of the 17 years of schooling. For women (not shown), the ratio was 13 out of 17. The pattern for the 11 income categories was similar.

Figure 1 Self reported health by years of schooling

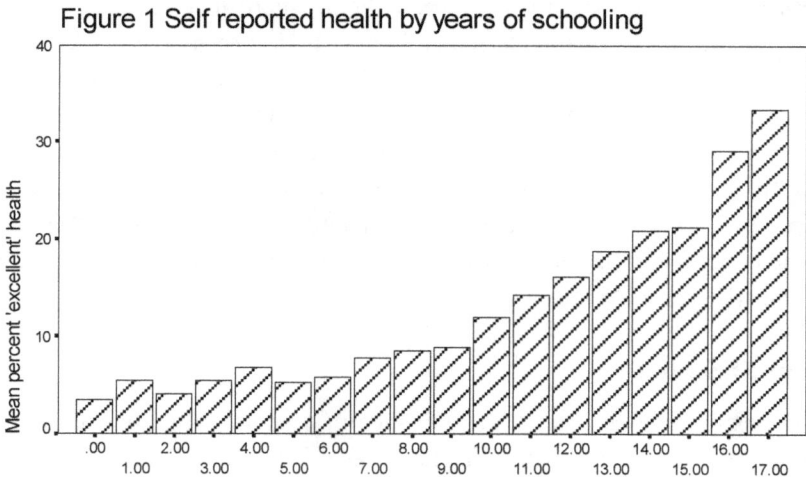

Simply knowing the existence of the monotonic relationship permits us to rule out a number of explanations. First, it is unlikely that observer bias could account for these distributions. A doctor might believe that educated people are generally healthy and build this fact into the final assessment, but it is unlikely that he/she would be biased in the complex way reflected in the distribution. Similar reasoning rules out the economic explanation. Economists might argue that money buys health care while education improves choices. But would this explanation account for the yearly increments? Given the emphasis that economists place on credentials as aids to job getting, they should expect plateaus of health status for primary, high school, and college graduates. It is hard to see how the economic explanation could handle finer gradations. Similar arguments can be made for most of the other proposed explanations that are reviewed below.

A second SES effect is the reduction of mortality from a variety of diseases. Syme and Berkman (1976) reported early on what may be called the "broad spectrum effect." Marmot et al. (1995:173) noted it in the Whitehall data: "A second provocative finding from the Whitehall Study is that social differentials in mortality apply to more of the major causes of death. This observation broadens the explanatory task beyond the one with which we began—the social gradient in coronary heart disease—to the social gradient in a wide variety of other diseases." (See also Dutton and Levine 1989:32; Anderson and Armstead 1995:213.)

A third feature is the "life course effect," the impact of SES on health in childhood (Lynch et al. 1994 (negative evidence); Mielck et al. 2002; Williams 1993; among many others) and after formal education has terminated (Haan et al. 1989). In the NHANES data, for example, both education and income continued to predict self-reported health for the elderly.

A fourth aspect of the SES effect is that the health gap between the rich and the poor is increasing. This issue is paramount in the British literature (Macintyre 1997), and studies in the US have shown similar trends (Feldman et al. 1989; Pappas et al. 1993). Pappas et al. (1993) list a number of possible explanations: a falling standard of living for those with high death rates, differential access to health care, and more health risks among the poorly educated. Additionally, they list the possibility that people with higher SES have adopted health lifestyles more rapidly.

The Impervious SES-Health Association

The fifth feature of the SES problem is that education and income continue to predict, despite controls on a wide range of possible determinants that are available in the NHANES instrument. This test emphasized biologically relevant variables because the biomedical explanation turns on them. The test is therefore more limited than the benchmark study by Ross and Wu (1995), which included work, psychological, and lifestyle mediators. These and similar comprehensive tests respond to the obvious criticism that researchers have simply not found the crucial intervening variables.

Robert and House (2000) believe the solution may require as many as twenty-five variables. The pressures on poor people are diverse and will require many different variables to account for the association. They recommend a broad array that covers the biomedical, environmental, behavioral, and psychosocial risk factors. Their strategy is quite empirical and seems to ignore the problem of explaining the gradient. The study of risk factors by Lynch et al. (1996) illustrates this recommended strategy. They introduced twenty-three mediating variables that reduced the excess relative risk to all-cause mortality by 85 percent for a sample of Finnish men, effectively dissolving the initial income association. In addition to age, the risk factors included fibrinogen, high-density lipoprotein cholesterol, serum Apo lipoprotein B, copper, hair mercury, systolic blood pressure, body mass index, etc., while the three behavioral factors included cigarette smoking, physical activity, and loneliness. Most of these are interpretable as physiological and conform to the reductionist format of the biomedical model. However, the authors provided no conceptual rule for selecting mediators, so it is unclear whether the result can be replicated. It is also possible that the relatively egalitarian income distribution in Finland may have made this a special case. The study nonetheless illustrates the possibility of dissolving the initial correlation within the biomedical format.

Ross and Wu (1995) suggest, among other possible mechanisms, that "education teaches a person to use his or her mind . . . (and this ability) may keep the central nervous system in shape the same way that physical exercise keeps the body in shape." This sounds like a different kind of physiological mechanism, much more cognitive. In view of the known functions of the immune system, it can only be partial, but it does illustrate the form that a single mechanism might take.

McEwen and Seeman (1999) have proposed the concept of "allostatic load" to account for the SES-health association. They define this process as the long-term elevation and/or intermittent responses to threats. It is similar to earlier ideas concerning the "general adaptation syndrome," but the physiology is worked out in more detail. If research demonstrates that measures of allostatic load can dissolve the connection of SES to health, and if the explanation can be expanded to account for the other SES effects, it has great potential.

Link and Phelan (1995) appear to break with the reductionist format in contending that SES continues to predict because there is a deeper sociological process at work. Instead of looking for a mechanism at the physiological level, they draw out the "resource" implications of SES. "The reason for such persistent associations . . . is that they involve access to resources that can be used to avoid risks. . . ." (1995:87). The risks turn out to be the familiar smoking, overeating, etc., along with some recent risks such as chemical pollutants, the pressures of social hierarchies, and the like. Still, these risk factors take us back to the reductionist format and the failure of risk factors to dissolve the SES/health correlation when they are used as mediators.

Link and Phelan might reply that their concept of resources is broader than risk avoidance because resources also help people to take advantage of new medical technologies and similar assets. Indeed, resources seem to be synonymous with competence in dealing with the problems of life. This broader conception is corroborated by their definition of resources "to include money, knowledge, power, prestige, and the kinds of interpersonal resources embodied in the concepts of social support and social network" (1995:87). This definition amounts to an elaboration of the meaning of socioeconomic status, and implies a long and undefined list of possible variables. For that reason, it is probably untestable.

Caldwell (1986, 1989) has introduced a psychological interpretation of the effect of schooling that parallels the two-step (resources then risk-avoidance) sequence that Link and Phelan propose. Caldwell rejects the relevance of quality and content of schooling in favor of a psychological transformation: "It is not so much what you learn or understand, but how you see yourself and others see you" (Caldwell 1989:106). He uses the term "autonomy" to summarize this personality development, and goes on to illustrate it with observations about the health socialization (via imitation) of school children, and the greater tendency of educated mothers to do something about a sick child, persisting until she gets satisfactory treatment.

These empirical and conceptual proposals for dissolving the SES-health association by identifying one or more mediators will probably continue, despite the expanded challenge of explaining the SES effects. Studies of health status have become more and more frequent in the last several decades (Kaplan 2001), and almost all of them include SES measures, if for no other reason than to eliminate the effect of what biomedical researchers once referred to as a "nuisance" variable. Oakes and Rossi (2003) counted 3,544 relevant articles published during 1990-99. If only 10 percent paid attention to the SES problem, that would amount to a tremendous effort. These studies have tested a wide range of possible mediators, and we may be sure that a successful test would have been noted. Instead, at least one review has concluded that the quest has been unsuccessful. Lanz et al. (1998:1703) report that "previous efforts to explain socioeconomic differences in mortality in a variety of sub-populations have found that strong differences remain after controlling for major lifestyle risk factors."

Do these arguments demonstrate that the direct effect of SES is impervious to dissolution? They do not. We cannot reject the possibility that someone will find at least one mediator and formulate a plausible interpretation. But in terms of probabilities, it is unlikely. With the possible exception of the broad spectrum effect on diseases, the SES effects have a strong social component. Yet these can be incorporated into the biomedical model only with difficulty.

The Biomedical Explanation

Although it is not generally recognized, the classical core of biomedical theory (the human organism with its immune functions surviving in a potentially threatening microparasitical environment) has now expanded to include social variables like SES. This expansion has occurred quietly because many researchers have not felt the need to explicate the relationship of these variables to the classical model, but it may be its most significant conceptual advance since the pioneering work of Pasteur and Koch. The expanded view has been codified and illustrated in the Berkman and Kawachi (2000) edited textbook, and more compactly in Berkman et al. (2000). Other writers, such as Pearlin and Schooler (1978), Williams (1998) and Kaplan (2000) have explicated parts of the model.

A simplified statement of the way SES has been incorporated into the biomedical model is that education, income, etc. "operate through" (Mosley and Chen 1984:34) the "proximate determinants" (as defined below) of health. In this model, the proximate determinants are central and fall into two categories: (1) host resistance and (2) environmental threats/insults. The first category has two major components, genetically determined and habits that build resistance. The second includes disease, injury, contamination (including smoking and smog), malnutrition, and possibly stress. All of these reflect the two defining features of the bio-medical model: Causal processes occur at the individual level and they are fundamentally physiological. The central feature of the classical theory is that it explains health as the organism's positive balance, with the help of science-generated defenses, against a constantly changing and potentially noxious environment (Dubos 1959; see also Pearlin and Schooler 1978). The organism is endowed with genetically determined defenses, but such host resistance can be enhanced by social determinants.

The other side of the coin is that the biomedical model prohibits a direct, unmediated relationship between SES and health. If a direct effect shows up empirically it must be a mistake of some kind because, according to the theory, the indirect conditioners like education are just that—they must work through the proximate determinants. They are not biological and cannot impact on the organism the way the biomedical model requires. Only a positive ratio of resistance to insults can bring about the biological state of wellness.

A Sociological Explanation

An alternative sociological explanation that claims to explain all five features of the SES puzzle begins with communities, and assumes that all communities, if they persist, develop a minimum capacity for "social problem-solving." They use three principal strategies: application of the specialized knowledge that is "stored" in the social division of labor; public debate that weighs the advantages and disadvantages of alternative policies; and, if these two strategies fail, looking at the problem from a fresh viewpoint—a "reform movement." Other less frequently employed strategies could be listed, but the important point here is that these concepts are sociological and were first developed in the study of communities.

This theory derives from Durkheim (1951, 1954), but not the side of Durkheim that has informed epidemiological research. That version may be called "societal attachment" theory and is a type of social psychology. The present explanation elaborates Durkheim's ideas about the structure of society. The term "structure" refers here to concepts and indicators that are system-wide and institutional (for the relevant community level). Structural theory eschews aggregated individual behaviors as well as any dichotomous mental categories that some have postulated. It also has a formal, content-free character, and uses interaction terms more centrally than other theories.

The first hypothesis of structural theory combines the three dimensions of problem-solving capacity with relevant "transaction organizations" to account for population health. Transaction organizations refers to factories, commercial firms, medical facilities, and the like that do the daily work of communities. Unlike the structural dimensions that are derived from theory, the transaction category refers to concrete organizations/agencies that cross the community boundary and whose efficacy must be assessed by trial and error. This fact is indicated by lower case letters: ph = $(S*o)$, where ph is an appropriate consensus-based measure of population health, S is one or more structural dimensions, and o is, in this case, one or more medical facilities. The $(S*o)$ interaction reflects "structural reinforcement," because it refers to the way structure can enhance the effects of transaction organization (and vice versa). In practice, however, transaction organization has little predictive power and it is usually dropped from the equation.

The more fundamental process is that participation in community problem-solving, even in the passive role of resident, improves health via moderated habits that optimize molar biological functions. Membership refers to institutionalized "citizenship" status, as indicated by voting, paying taxes, or owning property. If a community has a superior problem-solving capacity, the range of variation in behaviors like food and beverage consumption, emotional expression, work patterns, and mobility are moderated. This moderating effect facilitates molar optimization, which may be defined as a moving biological equilibrium adjusted to age and any disabilities.

The theory acknowledges threats to the community, starting with epidemics, and includes contemporary disruptions such as racism, forced migrations, and plant closings that undermine problem-solving. This formulation allows for the impact of microbial attacks on populations but focuses on the disruption of problem-solving capacity. Adding this term expands the formula to: ph = (C/t) when ph is an appropriate measure of population health, t is a problem that the community has identified as a threat and C refers to problem-solving capacity (a combination of the three structural dimensions).

This format holds for all levels of community, from the nation-state down to the household. In this form, the theory may be transposed to individuals. This version of structural theory makes the unconventional assumption that social personalities may be construed as "communities" (of roles and identities) that employ the same structural strategies and transaction organization found in the larger communities. Thus people continually make distinctions, they mentally debate issues in their "personal parliaments," and they develop solidarity in the form of a personal ideology and a sense of "career." At the individual level, transaction organization develops in response to environmental threats, and consists of the many activities, including work, membership in associations, ties of friendship and kinship, and physical activities by which people deal with daily problems. The list also includes the many habits, from hand washing to avoidances (of substances and to feared categories of people) that are thought to maintain health. In other words, the superior problem-solving person can be a locus of causality.

Application of the Structural Theory to the SES Effects

The structural model takes years of schooling as the primary component of SES and assumes that other indicators, such as income, occupation, or participation in clubs are weaker measures of the same underlying process. Years of schooling correlates strongly with health because it reflects all three problem-solving strategies. It is one of those lucky bureaucratically-produced measures, like the percent of the population living in cities, that almost always summarizes a multifaceted process. The basic understanding of specialization is reflected in the variety of subjects the students study and in the diversity of student backgrounds that forces everyone to make social distinctions very early in life. Pluralism is embodied in the verbal exchanges between students, teachers, and their families. Even in authoritarian schools, most children—minorities excepted—tend to argue freely outside the classroom. The third problem-solving strategy, social movements, is infrequent in schools, but the competition of teams is a partial substitute, because students quickly learn the importance of loyalty to leaders and teamwork in pursuing a defined purpose.

It should now be evident why an additional year of schooling tends to improve health. The learning (of the three problem-solving strategies) that is important to future health occurs if the student participates even minimally in the classroom and regardless of the content of instruction. Like language, of which they are an integral part, the major problem-solving strategies last a lifetime. They are remembered individually and collectively by the community and are available for use over everyone's life course. This interpretation implies that income and occupational level will usually be less strongly correlated with health status. Although affluent and/or occupationally well-placed families can usually gain entrance to subcommunities with stronger problem-solving capacity, the process does not always work. Education, in contrast, is a more direct proxy.

Strategies of social problem-solving can be learned elsewhere, of course. Family membership teaches the value of specialized knowledge and solidarity, but until recently most families did not allow much disagreement between children and parents. The contribution of the work environment varies widely with the organization of the workplace. More reliable as a "classroom" are voluntary associations that must allow freedom of expression because volunteers can always leave. Somewhat more remote is vicarious learning from the accounts of problematic situations in history books or the situation comedies on television.

How would structural theory explain the broad spectrum reduction in disease death rates? This finding presents a special problem because the definition of population health proposed above ruled out disease rates on the grounds that they are almost always organ-specific. Structural theory applies best to "global" rates like life expectancy. But a "cross-over hypothesis" is possible: The optimal biological functioning that is associated with superior problem solving strengthens the immune system. (See Seeman and McEwen 1996:464 for a similar statement.)

The widening health gap associated with educational levels is a result of people falling behind in the problem-solving skills needed for managing environmental threats, particularly in a changing economy. Rapid and dislocating social change, as has occurred in Eastern Europe (Hertzman et al. 1996) temporarily increases the proportion of people who experience difficulty in dealing with serious problems, especially loss of income. Eventually, the community-level problem-solving dimensions come into play and provide practices and technologies that less well-endowed individuals can appropriate for their personal situations. At the same time, the college-educated population, who typically come from superior problem-solving families, may have developed more capacity, especially in their (pluralistic) ability to take different perspectives. If so, they will be better equipped to handle the many new problems in a fast-moving world.

Therefore, the structural theory of population health provides a plausible account of the SES effects. But like the biomedical model it must deliver successful empirical tests that are consistent with its assumptions. If schooling is an all-purpose proxy for the three problem-solving dimensions, more precise measures of these should dissolve the initial correlation. What would such measures look like? There are probably many components of intelligence tests that focus on the ability to make practical distinctions. Likewise, inventories of role-playing capacity should capture the ability to engage in internal debates over personal "policies." A measure of the "mobilized personality" will be more difficult because it reflects a continuing process. But again, available tests could be adapted.

THE PERSISTENT DOCTOR-MORTALITY ASSOCIATION

Abstract: *The aim of the study is to explain the persistent but puzzling positive correlation of physicians per capita and mortality rates. This correlation has been reported many times since it was first observed in 1978. The explanation that is proposed and tested is that expanding urban-industrial regions attract an oversupply of doctors. Also, but independently, rural people migrate to urban-industrial areas where they suffer from the stress of adapting to urban-industrial life. Consequently, their death rates rise. Using data from the forty-seven Japanese pre-fectures, the explanation is examined by adding the appropriate test variable to a basic equation linking physicians per capita to mortality, net of income. The test variables dissolve or reduce the original cor-relation. The conceptual and empirical analysis exposes the positive correlation as spurious, but the availability of medical specialists had little impact on mortality rates in competition with the social and eco-nomic variables that were used as controls.*

In 1978, Cochrane, St Leger, and Moore called our attention to what has turned out to be a persistent positive association between physicians per capita and death rates. Their article examined environmental and dietary factors and these, together with GNP per capita, served as controls for the eighteen countries in their sample. Although they did not doubt that a causal interpretation was unjustified, their tests demonstrated a robust positive correlation. Accordingly, they called it "the anomaly which will not go away." Since then, this unexpected correlation has been replicated and expanded in a number of studies. These have distinguished the adult mortality rate from the infant mortality rate that Cochrane et al. (1978) emphasized, and they have also looked at a wider range of medical facilities, including hospitals. Several studies analyzed data for the less developed countries circa 1970–80. Wimberly (1990) found that change in health expenditures and in physicians per 100,000 population made no significant contribution to the prediction of life expectancy. In the equation for infant mortality, physicians made a significant but ("unex-pected") positive contribution, net of GNP per capita, school enrolment, and two economic dependency measures.

A review of studies of "avoidable" mortality and health services by Mackenbach et al. (1990:110) concluded that the associations of health care variables and mortality were "weak and inconsistent." The three studies that disaggregated the correlations found that half of the sixteen significant associations were positive—that is, the more health care, the higher the mortality rates. Similar findings have been reported by McKinlay and McKinlay (1977) and Jayachandran and Jarvis (1986). Going back in time, Williams (1993) has shown that the migration of peasants to the industrializing Glasgow region from about 1820 to 1870 had a marked negative impact on death rates, attributable to urban poverty and the destruction of the agrarian economy that they left. Given his purposes, he did not report the availability of physicians.

Clarke et al (1994) found no significant association in US counties between an index of primary care (physicians in general practice, family physicians, internists, pediatricians, obstetricians/gynecologists, and nurse practitioners) and infant mortality, when they controlled on a range of social-structural factors, including average income. Chen and Lowenstein (1985) found the expected negative correlation between physicians and infant mortality in their sample of sixty developing countries, but they did not control on GDP, so the association may not be final.

Cochrane et al. looked for but found no convincing explanation. They left it to others "to extricate doctors from this unhappy position" (1978:204). This article takes up their challenge. Even if no one believes that the positive correlation reflects causality, its existence is an embarrassment for the role of medical interventions in the biomedical explanation of health. Also, the exercise of demonstrating spuriousness should throw light on the role of medical facilities in comparison with the social and economic variables.

A New Explanation

The explanation proposed here is that, as compared with other regions, the expectation of opportunities in the growing industrial cities initially attracts an over-supply of doctors. Doctors in new regions enjoy fewer economies of scale, which means that they are more numerous as compared with the mature regions. These same industrializing cities attract rural immigrants whose health habits and social supports break down in the context of city life. Therefore, the places with the most doctors also have the highest death rates, but the two variables are associated only by common location.

The "industrializing context" explanation for the doctor-mortality correlation is general because such regions can be found in all parts of the world at one time or another. Still, it is epoch specific, because it assumes the existence of medical practices, particularly obstetrics and accident therapies, which are capable of decreasing the death rate.

Design of Research and Tests of Hypotheses

The analysis strategy should now be apparent. The first step is to replicate the positive doctor-mortality correlation, controlling on income per capita and any other relevant variables. Then a test variable—a measure of migration to industrializing regions—is added to the equation with the aim of dissolving, or at least reducing, the original correlation. With small samples, statistical significance may not be attainable, but the pattern of changes should conform to the accepted format for unmasking a spurious correlation. Regression analysis is the best technique for exploring this process, and it also shows the contribution of the control variables, the understanding of which is important in the regional industrializing process.

Japan since 1950 is a case of rural-urban migration from the countryside to the growing industrial cities in the southwest and northeast. The sample is limited to the forty-seven Japanese prefectures, but the quality of the data is high. A simple statistical analysis (not shown) cuts directly to the question at hand, postponing a detailed description of the variables. Thus male, age-adjusted mortality is negatively related to income per capita but positively related to physicians per 100,000, although neither is significant. When the dichotomy of mature versus growing regions is introduced in the second column, the regression coefficient for physicians drops to zero and the coefficient for the test region is significantly positive. In other words, the peripheral urban context accounts for the initial positive coefficient. In the context of the universe of prefectures, this shift is substantively significant.

Conclusion and Discussion

The research reported here confirmed the existence of the doctor-mortality correlation and dissolved the initial correlation. The doctor-death correlation is shown to be spurious, a conclusion that was never in doubt, but in the process of doing so the regional social context for death rates and the medical personnel who practice in the urban-industrial regions was clarified. Although both types of newcomers were responding to market forces in the growing cities, their activities were not articulated.

A larger question that is posed here has been raised earlier by McKeown (1976) and Alvarez-Dardet (1993). That question pertains to the efficiency of modern medicine. How can we explain that controlling on the test variable reduced the positive correlations for men, but did not reverse them? If doctors were, in fact, curing the workers, a lowered death rate should reflect it. Or should it? Medical interventions are weak causes compared with the general level of development. They are also weak, it seems, as compared with the stress of working in an industrializing region. The explanation of a spurious correlation raises deeper questions. Unlike the initial question, which was minor and almost amusing, the new questions are fundamental. They call attention to the effect of market forces in the delivery of medical care and the powerful effects of structure. Now, in addition to the effect of economic development on health (Japanese women the exception), we must take the negative impact of industrializing regions into account.

THE INCOME INEQUALITY-MORTALITY CORRELATION

Abstract: *This replication and reanalysis of an equivalent dataset to the one that Wilkinson and Pickett (2010) used in support of their hypothesis— that income inequality causes health and social problems in the American states—found, using regression analysis, that income inequality correlates with age-adjusted white mortality when per capita income is controlled but not when the control on location in the American South is added. This finding poses the question of what it is about the American South that undermines the initial inequality-low health correlation. Historical data indicate that the high Gini coefficient of income inequality in the southern and border states is a consequence of the aggressive policies of the landowning elites and the associated practices that keep the wages of black workers low. Further analysis supported the alternative hypothesis, that a smaller white population (and more nonwhites) in some states generates pervasive fear and lower population health. In short, the claim that income inequality causes health and social problems is spurious.*

Toward the end of their book, Wilkinson and Pickett (2010:268) offer a striking summary: "The relationships between inequality and the prevalence of health and social problems shown in the earlier chapters suggest that if the United States was to reduce its income inequality to something like the average of the four most equal of the rich countries (Japan, Norway, Sweden and Finland), the proportion of the population feeling that they could trust others might rise by 75 percent— presumably with matching improvements" (i.e., in the rates of health and social problems). This sentence is remarkable for its faulty comparison of the multi-racial US to four small ethnically homogeneous countries. It is even more remarkable because it implies a causal relationship between material inequality and a nine-indicator health and social problems composite score. Clearly, if this hypothesis is confirmed, it would quickly become the core theory linking social epidemiology and sociology.

Putting aside the rhetorical comparison, the task of a replication is to assess the validity of this claim and, if it proves unfounded, to offer an alternative explanation. Fortunately for researchers, Wilkinson and Pickett's book *The Spirit Level* (2010) reports the evidence that they and others have accumulated, and the methodology they used. It updates the paradigm from 1999, the publication year of a comprehensive collection of articles by Kawachi, Kennedy, and Wilkinson (1999), which includes the benchmark article on the American states by Kaplan, Pamuk, Lynch et al. (1996). So a replication can be based on this one book. That, at any rate, is the goal of this article, which uses one of their samples, the American states, for tests of hypotheses. After a summary and critique of the Wilkinson and Pickett research, this study introduces and tests an alternative "white status loss" hypothesis.

1. *The inequality-population health connection.* Wilkinson and Pickett argue that a single state-wide measure of income inequality, net of income, causes high levels of poor health and social problems. Their measure of inequality is the 1999 Gini coefficient of household income as calculated by the US Census Bureau. On the dependent side, they use the mean of the z scores for nine indicators: trust (reverse coded), life expectancy (reverse coded), teenage births, obesity, homicides, imprisonment rates, education (reverse coded), infant mortality, and mental illness. These nine indicators are a reasonable sample of health and social problems and the use of z scores is standard.

Wilkinson and Pickett report the correlation between income inequality and the index of problems with a scatterplot of the fifty states (2010: 22) that shows a strong association of .87 between the two variables. In subsequent chapters, they present comparable scattergrams for the separate indicators, again listing the correlation coefficients in the Appendix. In addition to these, they present a scatterplot for a crucial control variable, per capita income, that they must reject in order to make their case. Consistent with expectations, the income-health scatterplot shows little or no relationship.

The rejection of per capita income as an alternate predictor is in line with the standard practice for demonstrating causality when the analysis is limited to cross-sectional relationships. Lacking the all-purpose control that randomized clinical trials (and experiments in general) deliver, most researchers use multiple regression analysis to show that rival variables are not significantly correlated. But Wilkinson and Pickett believe they can do without an explicit rejection of other competing predictors. In their postscript (2010:285), they explain that they wish to present the simplest and most understandable picture of the correlation between inequality and health/social problems, so that readers can see the strength of the relationship for themselves. A second reason they give for avoiding controls is that, if they inadvertently hold constant a variable that is part of the causal chain, it would dissolve the initial relationship and mistakenly suggest that the independent and dependent variables were uncorrelated.

But these two reasons amount to an abrogation of current best practice for making causal claims on the basis of correlations, because controlling on plausible rival hypotheses is a requirement. Likewise, nobody is asking for a control on one or more of the mediating variables. Wilkinson and Pickett conclude their defense of the analysis strategy by noting that "many other studies of health and income inequality have controlled for poverty (and) average income," and others have examined the relationship of public spending, social capital, and the ethnic composition of populations (2010:286). Such an appeal to other studies seems to concede that the explicit rejection of rival hypotheses is part of the analytic task.

A second requirement for demonstrating causality is the theoretical identification of a plausible mediating process, one that is potentially measurable and which helps us to understand how the cause and effect are related. As noted above, Wilkinson and Pickett mention trust as a possible mediator. But the chapter entitled "How inequality gets under the skin" gives an extended discussion of their primary candidate, threats to the social self. They draw heavily (2010:38) on the Dickerson and Kemeny (2004) meta-analysis of 208 experimental studies that tested the impact of a threat to self-esteem/social status. The experimental results were particularly clear when the outcome of the treatment (usually a performance before judges) was beyond the subject's control. It is this kind of stress, they argue, that mediates the gamut of health and social problems (2010:43). Perhaps, but the experimental situation involved a direct diminution of self-esteem. Whether the subject's comparisons with other people would be equivalent is a separate question.

Wilkinson and Pickett then theorize that social relationships such as friendships and social cohesion protect against negative social evaluation and the stress it produces. Given this strong argument about the intervening mechanisms in small groups, their comment on size (2010:195) is puzzling: "With the exception of studies which looked at inequality in small local areas, an overwhelming majority of these tests (i.e., on larger units) confirmed the theory." These small local area studies sound like important negative cases that should be discussed. They highlight their findings for cross-national and cross-state samples, but not the small groups where one would think that invidious comparisons of status would be more frequent. As one seminar wit remarked, the one group where inequalities can be easily observed and emotions run high is in an academic department.

These empirical problems are troublesome for another reason—because they deflect our attention from the absence of a conceptual framework for these causal claims. What we have here occurs frequently in science when researchers find a strong correlation and then proceed to formulate an explanation. Such explanations stimulate other researchers to come up with competing theories. This possibility is reinforced by the discussion of ethnicity and inequality that Wilkinson and Pickett present. "Prejudice against minorities," they state, "might cause ethnic divisions to be associated with bigger income differences and, flowing from this, also with worse health and more frequent social problems" (2010:185). They note that in the American states income inequality is closely related to the proportion of African-Americans in the states' population, and that both the black and the white population show higher rates of poor health and social problems. They conclude that although inequality in ethnic divisions involves different processes, it should not be seen as an alternative explanation. But this paper will treat the ethnicity dimension as the basis for an alternative explanation, except that the crucial component is the status loss that whites perceive when the size and status of the minority population increases.

2. *Evidence of spuriousness in the inequality-health findings*: As noted, Wilkinson and Pickett's finding in support of the inequality-health proposition begins with a scatterplot for the states, followed by another which shows the lack of a relation between per capita income. This two-step analysis can be reproduced in a regression analysis as shown in Table 1. The correlation of the Gini coefficient of inequality and age-adjusted mortality for the white populations is a significant .40 when income is controlled. Table 1 substitutes age-adjusted white mortality for the nine-item index that Wilkinson and Pickett used, because downloading already-calculated and widely-used coefficients from the CDC (2012) Wonder file focuses on a standardized criterion. It also facilitates a comparison with a comparable multi-item measure (see below).

Table 1 Regression analysis of white and black mortality

Predictors	White mortality	White mortality	Black mortality
Gini00	.40*	.17	.21
Pcincome00	-.50*	-.32*	-.46*
South		.40*	
Pblack00			.36*
R2	.31	.39	.23

N=48 Alaska and Hawaii were dropped to keep the sample to the continental boundaries. N=43 for black mortality because of missing data. Data for this and subsequent tables were taken from the County and City Data Book Extra, 2002 unless otherwise noted. The table reflects a cross-section of 2000-2009.

White mortality=age-adjusted white mortality, 2004-07 (797; 684-968) (CDC Wonder File, Compressed mortality, 2012).

Black mortality=age-adjusted black mortality, 2004-07 (986; 591-1,187).

Gini00= Gini coefficient of income inequality (.45; .41-.50).

Pcincome00=income per capita, in 000s. (29k; 22k–42k).

Pblack00=percent black in all counties (11:1-37).

South=Alabama, Arkansas, Florida, Georgia, Louisiana, Mississippi, North Carolina, South Carolina, Tennessee, Texas, Virginia, plus the border states of Kentucky, Missouri and Oklahoma.

States with Gini coefficients of .47 or more, showing Gini coefficient and age-adjusted white mortality: Alabama .47, 937; California .47, 742; Connecticut, .48, 728; Florida, .47, 729; Louisiana, .48, 913; Mississippi, .47, 913; New York, .50, 740; Tennessee, .47; 911; Texas, .47; 799.

The second column adds another control variable, location in the American South. This is a standard control that most American researchers include in their analyses of the American states because it is known to affect almost all correlations one way or another. In this table, true to its reputation, the dichotomous variable is positively correlated .40 with the mortality criterion. But more important, it dissolves the original correlation, reducing it to a nonsignificant .17. Per capita income remains significant. The original correlation of .40 is accounted for (statistically) by the block of southern and border states listed at the foot of the table.

Although the prediction of age-adjusted black mortality is rarely mentioned in the income inequality studies, it is important in an analysis of the American states because the regression analysis of black mortality turns out to be a weaker version of that for the whites. As before, the Gini coefficient becomes nonsignificant. The same regression was run on the non-South states (not shown). As expected, it showed no significant coefficients with white mortality, even though some of the states have high Gini coefficients. That result prompted an alternative partition of the sample separating the states with a Gini coefficient of .47 or greater. These states are listed at the foot of the table where six of the nine are located in the South. But the other three (California, Connecticut, and New York) have high income inequality and low levels of mortality, thereby contradicting the inequality-mortality hypothesis. An adequate explanation must deal with these deviant cases.

3. *Explaining the inequality-health correlation*: The finding in Table 1, where a control on a historically distinctive region accounts for the correlation, raises the question of whether the inequality-social problems correlation is spurious (Matthews 2000). If so, we must look elsewhere for the real cause. Moreover, if the causal interpretation of the inequality-health correlation is spurious, the Gini coefficient must be adventitiously associated with the social organization in the American South. The history of this region offers a starting point, because former plantation regions typically maintain the ethnically distinct land-owning families and the cheap non-white labor pool (Tomaskovic-Devey and Roscigno 1997; Wright 1986:156ff). On the wealthy end of the scale, the state legislatures keep unions weak and taxes low (only three of the fourteen southern states were above the median per capita taxes as listed in the 2004 County and City Data Book Extra). Additionally, since World War II, Southern senators have a history of aggressive lobbying in Congress for subsidies (Wright 1986:261ff) that probably favored the wealthy elites. The increase in Southern support for the Republican party, which began as early as 1948 (Lamis 1999:2), probably facilitated such Congressional favoritism. In particular, the spread of defense industries to the South after World War II brought new investment opportunities for the wealthy investors (Grantham 1994:270ff). The graph of rising inequality for the US in Wilkinson and Pickett (2010:240) coincides with this period.

A factor analysis of items that are similar to those used in the Wilkinson and Pickett study generated two factors that bear on the question of what the criterion variable(s) are measuring. The first factor is defined by high "loadings" (correlations of .50 or higher with the whole cluster) for the percent of households with high incomes, the median value of homes, the number of doctors per capita, and the percent with some college education. The second factor is defined by the percent of the adult population that is unemployed, the percent of families with incomes below the poverty line, the percent disabled, the violent crime rate, and the percent without health insurance. The label "poverty" fits this factor.

The two factors are independent because the varimax rotation, a standard default, was used. Both factors are significantly correlated, with opposite signs, with white mortality, and the R^2 is .51. Factors like these are typically used as measures of socioeconomic status, which is a well-known predictor of health outcomes.

Table 2 Factor matrix of indicators of poverty and affluence in the U.S. states

Indicator	Affluence	Poverty
Pcinck00	.89	
Mdvalk00	.88	
Phypht00	.86	
Pcoll00	.79	
Punemp00		.88
Ppovfam00		.81
Pdisab00		.80
Rviolc00		.70
Pnoinsur00		.60
Range	-1.7 – 2.1	-1.6 – 2.5
R^2 explained	.37	.35

Pcinck00 = per capita income, 000s, 2000. (29; 22-24).
Mdvalk00 = median value of housing, 000s, 2000. (115; 72-216).
Phypht00 = physicians per 100,000 population, 2000. (208; 142-327).
Pcoll00 = percent with some college education, 2000. (25; 15-35).
Punemp00 = percent labor force unemployed, 2000. (5.4; 4-7).
Ppovfam00 = percent families classified as poor, 2000. (8.8; 4-16).
Pdisab00 = percent population classified as disabled, 2000. (19.2; 15-24).
Rviolc00 = rate of violent crime, 2000. (421;81-812).
Pnoinsur00 = percent families lacking health insurance, 2000. (13; 6-22).

A test of the white status loss hypothesis: This research nominates "white status loss" as a powerful cause that explains the differential mortality rates in the states. There is a growing literature (Maharidge 1996; Schrag 2010; Swain 2002; Walters 2003) on the "impending minority status" of white populations in the US. The white population of California has now fallen below 50 percent and the urgent attempts of this new "minority majority" to maintain its position by limiting the growth of the nonwhite populations, particularly the Latinos, are well documented. Maharidge (1996) argues that California's recent series of propositions were all designed, at least in part, to limit or block the growth and welfare of the minority population. Proposition 13 (1978) capped real estate taxes for seniors, resulting in the underfunding of schools, parks, and police that minorities depended on; Proposition 14 (1964) killed the state's fair housing law; a 1986 law declared English as the state's official language; Proposition 184 (1994), the three strikes prison law, targeted minorities; Proposition 187 (1994) denied public services (especially hospitals and schools) to illegal immigrants; and California's Civil Rights Initiative (1996) ended affirmative action in all aspects of state government one year after the state university system had terminated affirmative action for students. Following California's lead, other states passed similar laws, sometimes simply copying the language of the original. The rapid diffusion of these laws suggests that the implications of the demographic shift are understood by the white population as a loss of historical status, and Maharidge's extensive interviews revealed widespread fears on that score. Not surprisingly, the embattled whites have increasingly joined "white nationalist" associations (Swain 2002) once the older "white supremacy" groups had been discredited or outlawed.

A theoretical point that should be made explicit is that the structural theory that helps to interpret white status loss defines "community" as a multifunctional group with a concern for the welfare of its members (Selznick, 1996). This definition applies to nation-states, provinces, villages, and on down to the household. It is further assumed that communities act as units in their efforts to adapt to a changing and sometimes threatening environment. These assumptions undergird the hypothesis that the whites in U.S. communities may react with "collective stress" when faced with an existential threat. All the members of the community feel the stress and the effect becomes an emergent property of the community. When such stress continues for months or years, it can disrupt the physiology of all or most of the inhabitants (Seeman and McEwen 1996; also Brunner 1997), increasing the likelihood of premature death. The possibility of something like collective stress occurring in communities has been noted by the methodologist Diez-Roux (1998) and by the philosopher of science Bunge (2009), among others. Thoits'

(2010) comprehensive review of the individual stress literature hints at the possibility of collective stress. In contrast to the reductionist path (via individual behavioral risks), the causal path here is direct.

Table 3 tests the hypothesis that white status loss causes high mortality rates in the states. The upper part of the table uses the percent of the African-American population and the percent Hispanic as indirect measures of the shrinkage of the white population. Percent black predicts both white and black mortality, supporting the white status loss hypothesis. One explanation of this double impact is that weak governments, which are frequent in the South, depress the health of the whole population via collective stress.

Table 3 Regression analysis of mortality using ethnicity predictors

Predictors	Aamw0407	Aamb0407
Pblack00	.37*	.48*
Phispanic00	-.27 (.06)	-.19
R^2	.22	.28
Pwhite00	-.41*	-.31*
Pnatborn00	.10	.44*
R^2	.14	.24

Aamw and aamb=age-adjusted mortality, averaged over 2004-07, for non-Hispanic whites and blacks, CDC Wonder file. N for regression for pblack00 is 43 due to missing data. For pwhite00, N =45 after deleting two outliers with high white death rates and high percent white. (W. Virginia and Kentucky). Pnatborn00=percent population born in state (64; 25-83).

A measure of white population change did not predict. That finding is negative evidence against the white status loss hypothesis, because a shrinking white population is probably more evident to the local whites, and it is more likely to be interpreted as a threat. The percent Hispanic was only weakly correlated with white mortality and the sign was negative. It may be that the two unexpected signs for the Hispanic correlation reflect the recent migration of this ethnic group to affluent states that need workers for their industries.

The lower rows of Table 3 use the straightforward percent white as the main predictor along with percent native born, which controls on the migration status of the black and white population. Percent white predicts lower mortality for both blacks (-.31) and whites (-.41), but only after deleting two outliers—West Virginia, with a high percent white and a high white mortality rate, and Kentucky, with the same pattern. These two states probably have a high percent of the white population with low SES. Percent native born predicts higher mortality for blacks only, reflecting their lower mobility out of the South.

4. *Conclusion and discussion*: This reanalysis of state data that is comparable to that which Wilkinson and Pickett (2010) presented in support of the association of income inequality and health/social problem measures found that controlling on a state's location in the American South dissolved the initial relationship and raised the question of spuriousness. The alternative hypothesis proposed and tested here is that the threat of white status loss explains population health differentials. This type of unmanaged threat, which in this case is existential, is hypothesized to generate collective stress and higher rates of mortality.

Although Wilkinson and Pickett do not discuss them, the exceptional states (high inequality and low mortality) like California, Connecticut, and New York, must be explained too. Structural theory postulates greater organizational capacity in these states for accommodating the growth of minorities. The possibility of a "capacity" dimension that interacts with the threat was not investigated in this study for lack of cases and capacity indicators. It is, however, a central variable in the structural theory that provides the foundation for the white loss hypothesis (Young, 2012).

Where does that leave the Wilkinson and Pickett paradigm? If the present critique holds, the inequality-mortality causal claim faces a special challenge because, aside from the differential supporting evidence, the alternative white status loss hypothesis is a parsimonious sociological explanation. By contrast, Wilkinson and Pickett explain the impact of inequality by an economic variable that must be mediated by a complex social-psychological process that departs from the conventional meaning of income inequality.

The two hypotheses do have something in common, however. Both start their causal sequences with a "structural" concept. Income inequality and white status loss are both community-level processes and they predict outcomes that are best interpreted as emergent properties. Other macro social hypotheses exist, to be sure, but these two dramatically illustrate the advantages of shifting to a community unit.

A SOCIAL PROBLEMS PUBLIC HEALTH?

Abstract: *The biomedical theory that guides the work of public health departments does not explain the health impacts of social problems like teenage pregnancies, unemployment, or ethnic conflict, but public health departments are increasingly concerned with such problems. Current theory is still based on pathogens. But the fit is less than perfect and an alternative sociological model does better for the non-pathogen cases. It focuses on weak community problem-solving, "collective stress," and negative health outcomes. This type of theory suggests the possibility of a new branch of public health, one that focuses on social problems.*

To judge by actual practice, public health professionals have already answered the question in the title, but in a surprising way. Yes, social problems cause population health differentials, but there is no need for a new branch of public health. The established discipline can encompass social problems and, in fact, it already has. A textbook (Berkman and Kawachi 2000) contains chapters on socioeconomic status, discrimination, income inequality, job loss, social isolation, and the cohesion of communities. Likewise, the annual meetings of the American Public Health Association include sessions on a wide range of problems and solutions—everything from inequality to human rights. A key date is 1985, when the Surgeon-General of the U.S. held a forum on "Violence as a Public Health Problem" that put the government's stamp of approval on the study of social problems such as violence. (Prothrow-Stith and Weissman 1999:138). The fact that the pathogen-based biomedical theory does not cover these problems seems not to concern public health professionals.

Despite its widespread acceptance, the biomedicine paradigm does not explain all the causes of death. In fact, it leaves half of them unexplained (McGinnis and Foege 1993; also Mokdad et al. 2004). These researchers found, on the basis of an inventory of the accumulated biomedical research, that the top ten risk factors (smoking, excessive consumption, inactivity, alcohol, microbial agents, toxic agents, firearms, sexual behavior, motor vehicles, and illicit drugs), in that order of importance, account for no more than 50 percent of annual deaths. What accounts for the other 50 percent? McGinnis and Foege do not claim that the medical literature has exhausted all possible causes, and most of their readers will assume that biomedical research will eventually close the explanation gap. At the end of their replication, Mokdad et al. (2004) discuss other possible causes, such as unknown pollutants, genetics, and a range of social factors, such as lack of access to primary care, poverty, low education, and ethnicity. But many of these factors depart from the biomedical paradigm and are not named in the medical literature. McGinnis and Foege comment that the three leading causes of death (smoking, diet/inactivity, and alcohol) "are all rooted in behavioral choices" (1993:2211) but, in fact, all ten of the causes they list, with the possible exception of microbial and toxic agents, are embedded in individual behaviors. Ironically, their search for "actual" causes led them to social factors.

This essay begins with the distinction between wellness, in the sense of absence of disease, and vitality, defined as abundant energy and mental alertness. In other words, the sickness-wellness and low-high vitality dimensions are separated. It is the latter type of health that structural theory claims to explain, although there may be cross-links to wellness. Unfortunately, measurement is not so clear. A rate such as age-adjusted mortality can reflect both sickness and low vitality. Even so, the distinction is useful in theoretical discussions.

A Structural Explanation of the Health Consequences of Social Problems

The best way to introduce the structural explanation of health is to start with the sketch of the dominant biomedical explanation. It is now more than a theory of germs and disease. It moves from behavioral risk factors, such as those listed above, to various mediation processes, such as stress and social support. This causal sequence determines the vulnerability of the human body to the risk factors and the many ways that malfunctioning physiology can cause death. Biomedical theory focuses on individual processes, although the literature (Galea 2007; Schoeni, House, Kaplan and Pollack 2008) now includes a discussion of the macro causes of the distribution of risk factors. It is also strongly committed to interventions, either by changing the risk factors or by adjusting the malfunctioning physiology. But despite this expansion, the biomedical paradigm is still strongly focused on diseases. Finding a cure and treating a deadly disease is still the guiding principle of government expenditures and the training of doctors.

The ideal public health intervention is some variant of John Snow's pump handle that, once it was removed, stopped the spread of cholera in a London neighborhood by keeping the local residents from drinking contaminated water (Lomas 1998). A single change protected all the residents against a range of diseases. Later investigation expanded the list of contaminants to include animal droppings. The microbial agents were not identified until later, but decisive interventions became the exemplar. It is well to remember, though, that while Snow's action helped in the short term, the water remained contaminated. It took London many decades and a huge investment to build a sewerage system that permanently protected the drinking water.

Now, in addition to microbial agents which, according to the McGinnis and Foege study, explain only 4 percent of annual deaths, we have a longer list; and they all have strong behavioral components that generate media campaigns and personal counseling that mostly boil down to the command "stop it!" Compounding the problem is the way these behavioral risks are embedded in customs and lifestyles that resist change. As the Michigan team (Kaplan, Ranjit, Burgard 2008) learned in the course of its analysis of racial discrimination, the recommended social changes tend to be intertwined and often ineffective. Very quickly, social epidemiologists find themselves doing political science or sociology with little theory to guide them.

And then there is the unexplained 50 percent of annual deaths that McGinnis and Foege (1993) discovered. The absence of surprised commentary with respect to this finding can only be explained by the tacit assumption that medical science will eventually find the causes. Meanwhile, one is tempted to label the unknown causes as the burdens of old age, although that is not the type of explanation that the study accepted. For many investigators, that is still better than opening the Pandora's box of investigating macro level (i.e., supra individual) social risks like unemployment, ethnic conflict, street gangs, and domestic violence. Why is there so much resistance to expanding research on these possible causes? For one thing, they involve so much variation that they seem like another universe. A deeper point of resistance is the fear of giving up the assumption that health is an individual phenomenon, even when it is aggregated up to units like provinces and nation-states. This assumption of "methodological individualism" has permeated Western society since the early philosophers introduced it. It is on this fundamental point that structural theory parts company with economics and most of sociology. Structural theory rejects Margaret Thatcher's (reported) claim that "there is no such thing as societies; there are only men and women," by reversing the quote: there are no such thing as men and women (in this theory); there are only societies.

The rejection of the individual unit of analysis also implies the rejection of "institutions," when these are defined as complexes of rules and practices that guide individual behavior. If one accepts the community unit and relations between levels, then there is no need for the "individual in society" paradigm that was imported from Europe after World War II. An additional reason for rejecting institutions is that, in the last analysis, they cannot be measured in ways that permit tests of hypotheses. They are ambiguous, constantly changing, and so intertwined with each other that reliability and validity are undermined. This "falsifiability" requirement of social theory is difficult to impose but it is still a worthwhile guide to rigorous research.

Where does that leave us? First, structural theory rejects the current attempt to link "policies" to behavioral risk and thence to mortality and sickness rates. These policies are embryonic institutions and the supporting paradigm is still the institutional picture of the individual and society. This rejection means that testing hypotheses about the impact of medical facilities and the many other interventions implied by the germ theory is not relevant for the unexplained 50 percent. What is possible, according to structural theory, is applying the ph=C/t ratio hypothesis, where ph is an appropriate measure (for the community level under study), t is a serious threat to the community, and C is social problem-solving capacity, in the sense of an appropriate combination of the application of specialized knowledge, debating alternative courses of action and, less frequently, a reform movement. A familiar example for urban residents is the minority pressure for housing that threatens the longtime residents. The knowledge of other "invasions" permeates city life and constitutes an existential threat to a neighborhood.

This structural theory of population health may be compared to the Darwinian triad of mutation, environmental selection, and reproductive superiority. An obvious difference is that structural theory nominates an appropriate measure of population health as its universal criterion. In other words, it substitutes a qualitative criterion for the Darwinian quantitative measure. Qualitative measures of health, especially those that take disability days into consideration, are generally acknowledged as more appropriate for humans. Structural theory reformulates the impact of the environment by calling attention to the many socially defined threats. The social identification of threats, which depends on human language, is an adaptive advantage for the community. Like the Darwinian paradigm, however, structural theory does not specify which threats are serious. It is fundamentally different in postulating a ratio instead of a random mutation/ environmental connection, and it assigns adaptive capacity to the community as a whole instead of the aggregated individuals of orthodox Darwinian theory.

Applied Implications of Structural Theory

The capacity/threat interaction hypothesis claims that an increase in capacity relative to threat improves population health. Conversely, a reduction in capacity and/or the appearance of a more serious threat reduces population health, so the two variables can be viewed as social levers which improve health. But a closer examination of these variables raises questions. Threats tend to be random from the point of view of the community. Putting aside the vagaries of nature, the economies of communities at all levels and, increasingly, the nations of the world, are frequently beset by downturns. Likewise, the migrations of people are thought to pose an existential threat to the inhabitants of advanced nations. Warfare and similar aggressions continually explode. Longterm prevention of these threats usually requires the efforts of superordinate communities that are in a position to control events at lower levels. A strong national government can increase the capacity of the subordinate levels by subsidizing cities, authorizing local legislatures, or fostering reforms. Many of these practices diffuse from metropolitan centers. That leaves the question of whether a community level like the county can increase capacity by itself without superordinate help. From time to time that seems to happen, but such indigenous increases in capacity seem to be mostly unpredictable.

The Structural Dilemma

We are left with a structural dilemma. On the one hand, shifts in the interaction ratio are hypothesized to cause population health differentials. On the other, the components of the ratio are difficult and, perhaps, impossible to change. They just happen, and responsible community leaders are left to pick up the pieces or to reap the rewards. Of course, these community leaders would strongly deny that their work consists of random efforts. When they meet, formally or informally, they are constantly discussing strategies and initiatives, and some of these are enacted into law or administrative rearrangements. How could these efforts not make a difference? Structural theory acknowledges the everyday role of "transaction organization" but denies that the problem-solving which they embody is causal for population health. That role is left to structure.

If we accept the difficulty of changing structural variables, we are left with the lesser task of harnessing the ongoing structural dynamics, much as space travel uses gravitational forces. A familiar social example is schooling. Universal education is not usually seen as health protection, but the structural interpretation of how schooling enhances the average level of individual problem-solving capacity implies such a role. The exposure to a wide range of knowledge and skills, the arguments among students that typically arise both in the classroom and on the playground, and the occasional reforms in programs enhance the level of problem-solving capacity of the students, regardless of what they learn from the standard curriculum.

Applying the structural format to individuals is unconventional but informative. Transaction organization at the individual level is as varied and changing as it is for all community levels. Finding long-term employment, a spouse and a community of residence are primary concerns. As for relations with others, we now have a term, "networking," that captures this continuing and ubiquitous transaction activity. Likewise, terms like "health practices" and lifestyles abstract much of the individual's concern with personal health. Structural theory would simply point out that human groups have been experimenting with such practices since the beginning of social organization. The contribution of science is recent.

A less prosaic example is the way social movements that incorporate minorities into the larger society may improve their average health. When African-Americans achieved an improved status as a consequence of the civil rights movement (Cooper et al. 1981) they were open to a wide range of initiatives. Much trial and error took place, and it is likely that many black families were able to improve their job prospects. Likewise, they watched situation comedies on television that included black people and conveyed many habits and orientations of the wider middle class.

That said, there is one option that future research should explore. That is the possibility of institutionalizing structural pluralism in regions that have already moved in that direction, building on the momentum. Professionals who aspire to change structure should examine the region closely in the aftermath of a broad social movement, with the aim of finding any unrealized potential. Given the continuing emphasis on minority inclusion, it might be possible to improve their position across all counties and increase the level of structural pluralism.

A Social Problems Public Health (SPPH) Program

The starting assumption for a sociologically grounded branch of public health is that social problems are different from biological pathogens and cannot be managed in a biological framework. Even if the sociological theory proposed here is not successful, another will replace it and two branches of public health, perhaps with contrasting names, will emerge. The growth of a SPPH organization would compete with pathogen-based public health in two respects. It would force pathogen-based public health to clarify its own theory and construct rigorous tests for the gaps that still exist. Such clarification would automatically improve the precision of public health statements, moving them from the goal of improving an amorphous "health status" to a more precise "disease reduction." At the same time, the many risk factors would be recognized as ad hoc, and the discipline could realize that its theory is grounded in the individual's attributes and, therefore, ill-equipped to deal with community-level processes.

How would a social problems public health function? The initial task of constructing an inventory of variables and research findings on the connection between social problems/threats and health could be undertaken by a few specialists scattered in departments and institutes around the US. The actual materials could be organized in computer files and transferred electronically. A special task for the storage and inventory function of the SPPH network is to identify previous research that is interpretable in structural terms.

A second task for this embryonic network is to identify opportunities for exploratory replication. The first part of this task could be routinely accomplished by repeating research initially undertaken on a given community level on other levels. Moving from counties to states or vice versa is a typical pattern, but structural theory works with communities at all levels. For households there are many studies that are interpretable in structural terms. The responses from a sample of households may contain measures of household complexity, husband-wife debates on family matters, and "reform movements" embodied in separations or divorces.

Beyond building up the research infrastructure, what kinds of practical interventions does the theory suggest? A popular strategy is simply to follow the lead of other communities and attempt to introduce already tested practices for managing particular problems. The programs for assisted living residences for seniors that are rapidly diffusing in villages and cities are a current example. A state-wide inventory should indicate the types of agencies that comparable counties have acquired. Some of these could become candidates for imitation. In the broader framework of community ecology, these adoptions and modifications of dedicated agencies reflect the trial and error process that all communities pursue.

A type of problem on which there are many studies is the impact of ethnic succession in large cities. Wilson and Taub's (2006) book *There Goes the Neighborhood* is a relatively recent example. In this context, we can speculate that the reduction in the size of the white population has been accelerated in part by the increased freedom and movement of minorities that the civil rights movement stimulated. In particular, minorities are moving into the suburbs as they attain middle-class status.

Natural experiments like these are infrequent, but with the aid of theory and statistics more and more of them will be identified. It is likely, also, that the increased interest in population health by governments at all levels of community will reinforce the efforts of dedicated researchers. It seems increasingly evident that, in addition to providing for the economic security of its citizens, governments will accept the responsibility of maintaining high levels of health. Competition in the expanding global capitalism requires this. But it will not happen because of increased investments in conventional healthcare. Enhanced public health is probably the only way to improve population health, and even there the guidance of the biomedical paradigm is almost exhausted. The growth of a social problems public health may be just in time.

SECTION 4
STRUCTURAL ECOLOGY

Overview

The first article in this group has been renamed (from the original "Population Health as a Fundamental Criterion of Social Ecology") to emphasize its role as a summary statement of the theory that previous articles have dealt with piecemeal. Although I have not done a systematic survey, the formula in this article may be the first and only law in sociology. It is also backed by a theory that explains why the law works. The formula ph=C/t or, in words, improved population health is caused by a positive ratio of problem-solving capacity in relation to serious threats to the community. It is Darwinian in using three "variables" to summarize a universal process that covers many different instances. Two of these variables, population health and threats, are well specified and/or they depend on the community to identify threats. In this they are like "coping" in psychological theory that moves directly from a common-sense term to indicators. By contrast, Capacity is defined theoretically and provides guidelines for valid measurement. Despite the hybrid character of the formula, it provides a conceptual map of the interrelations of these variables and the possibility of empirical tests.

The second paper in this group, the analysis of data on the 105 Kansas counties, was undertaken to demonstrate the superiority of the modern strategy of combining theory with empirical tests. It claims to be intrinsically superior to the product of even a talented journalist. In addition, this article introduces a simple method for testing the ratio interaction hypothesis of community adaptation. In the absence of direct measures, county urban status was used as a measure of capacity and "white status loss" is the indicator of threat. This approximation of a negative ratio was hypothesized to predict the high level of conservative voting that is typical of the nativistic reaction that structural theory predicts when the ratio interaction is negative, that is, when capacity is weak compared to the threat.

The third and fourth papers in this group diverge from the small community emphasis of the other studies. Both are examples of nativistic reactions, and they illustrate the scope of the ratio interaction hypothesis. The analysis of the Islamic Counter-Reformation deals with historical data to show the similarity between the present human rights threat to Muslim countries and the Islamic reaction, as compared to the Protestant Reformation-Catholic Counter Reformation in the fifteenth century. The title of the paper reflects this historical leap. The last article, dealing with qualitative sociology, introduces a rhetorical shock with its claim that one branch of the social sciences exemplifies a nativistic movement. Taken together, the articles in this section imply that nativism can erupt whenever a weak community faces a long-term decline. In the modern world, that is an increasingly frequent combination.

A FUNDAMENTAL DYNAMIC OF SOCIAL ECOLOGY

Abstract: *This essay elaborates the common insight that "strong" communities respond more successfully to serious threats than "weak" communities, and it also claims that the successful communities will have better population health rates. It nominates an appropriate measure of population health as the criterion of success, and advances a universally applicable concept of strength, conceptualized as institutionalized problem-solving capacity, based on three components: the application of specialized knowledge, open debate on policy alternatives, and mobilization behind reformers and reform movements. The community is the locus of causality and it is assumed that communities attempt to adapt to threats by problem-solving. The threat-Capacity dynamic is explained by a combination of neo-Darwinian and neo-Durkheimian theory. Three kinds of applications support its plausibility.*

A research report by Wilson and Taub (2006) echoes the still relevant "Chicago School" of social ecology in describing the ethnic competition in four Chicago neighborhoods. Wilson and Taub draw on Hirschman's (1970) conceptualization of "exit, voice and loyalty" to describe the individual reactions to threats from encroaching ethnic groups. It is somewhat surprising, then, that in their last chapter, the authors look back on the neighborhoods and suggest a structural formulation: "In general, when residents perceive that in-migration presents a threat to their neighborhood, they will react either by exiting or by joining forces with other neighbors to resist the change. The stronger the social organization of the neighborhood, the more likely it is that local residents will select the 'voice' (i.e., defensive organization) option and take steps to keep the area stable."

Residents are more likely to choose the "exit" option when they feel that a neighborhood's resources, including the social organization of the community, are insufficient to stem the tide of ethnic change (2006:177-78). It is probable that many versions of this same insight are scattered through the literature. The problem is how to conceptualize this social ecological proposition. Although borrowed concepts like the "web of life," "invasive species," "succession," "accommodation," and the like are helpful, they are misleading in the social context. Rather, the common insight of threat-capacity interaction can lead to a more precise and general statement: as compared to weak groups, the members of strong communities are more likely to survive and even thrive in the face of serious threats. This statement leaves "strong" and "weak" undefined and the criterion of success unspecified. It is vague about threats, although they are thought to be "serious." But these deficiencies set the task for sociological theory. It must supply the definitions, the assumptions, and the relational form that will make this statement plausible and testable.

Defining the community as the unit of adaptation implies that environmental threats, especially from other communities, are frequent. Communities are constantly engaged in monitoring threats and responding to them, depending on their organizational capacity. This description also holds for their reactions to the physical and biological environment where, without purpose or intent, nature imposes earthquakes, climate fluctuations, abrupt shifts in resources, and the like. Many of these turn out to be the problematic by-products of earlier human activities, but it is the immediate threat that activates defensive action.

The Darwinian perspective is inescapable in dealing with the threat-response dynamic, but it must be transposed to human, language-using communities. Instead of "mutations," the formulation proposed here uses a new definition of strong and weak organization that generates specific strategies. Instead of environmental selection, it focuses on community-defined threats. The Darwinian criterion of "reproductive superiority" is replaced by "population health." Then the formula becomes:

$$ph = C/t$$

where ph is a measure of population health, as described below, t is a serious threat, and C refers to problem-solving capacity. The upper and lower case letters distinguish the theory derived from the purely empirical terms. Population health refers to a family of measures that is supported by a consensus among researchers and administrators, while Capacity is a concept derived from theory. Threats must be empirically identified for a given region and community level.

The formula also applies to individuals. Specialized knowledge and skills are easily measured with a vocabulary test, and the contestation over policies translates to mentally "weighing the alternatives." Reform movements occur from time to time when people change their housing, jobs, or spouses. So interpreted, the individual takes its place in structural theory as a special kind of community, with the advantage that there are many surveys and psychological studies that may be reworked for testing structural hypotheses.

The dynamic that the formula summarizes is fundamental, because capacity and threat reflect the relationship of community and environment, while population health stands as the criterion of success. The formula is fundamental in the sense of being comprehensive: It is unlikely that an additional variable of this scope exists. Variables such as population characteristics, energy consumption, technology, political organization, and the like are either subsumed by capacity and threat or they serve as ad hoc control variables that sharpen the figure-ground outlines of the phenomena. The formula is also fundamental in the sense that specific hypotheses can be derived from it. One such corollary is that unmanaged external threats (e.g., a plant closing) generate "internal" threats (e.g., unemployment) at lower levels of community, especially the household, and these, in turn, generate a range of deviant behaviors, as individuals attempt to solve their problems by trial and error. These deviant behaviors almost always disrupt the health habits that people have learned in the family and from the wider ethnic group. When this happens, biological functioning becomes suboptimal, and vitality in the sense of energy and mental alertness is reduced, causing early death.

A final question posed by this overview is whether or not the proposed formula is simply a special case of the general Darwinian explanation. The specification of population health as the criterion of community adaptation, for instance, is well within the Darwinian framework. Likewise, the identification of threats by community leaders could be construed by strict Darwinians as randomized selection, despite all the thought that might go into it. What about the application of capacity? Is it really so blind that it must be considered equivalent to mutations? Some may think so and point to the trial and error that the application of capacities involves. But another look at these components suggests that the reason that capacity will work in this theory is that it is a social version of the scientific method. The survey of specialized information that communities make in trying to solve the problem is comparable to the specification of alternative hypotheses in a scientific experiment, and the arguments over the best solution amount to a rough adjudication process. Reforms are the social equivalent of "paradigm shifts" in scientific work.

Specifying the Threat-Capacity-Response Dynamic

Structural ecology, as this version may be called, takes the community, defined as a multifunctional group that is concerned with the welfare of its members (Selznick, 1996), as the locus of causality for explaining "population health." By this definition, communities range from the household unit to the nation-state, a spectrum that includes units like counties and organized ethnic groups. At each level, community representatives are expected to deal with the "problems" that appear, including the serious issues that come to be defined as "threats." These community levels tend to form nested hierarchies wherever a country has developed far enough to benefit from a complex hierarchical interlocking. When the vertical nesting is defined by law, as is typically the case for administrative districts, the rights and duties of each level define the levels of causality and the relations between levels. So defined, communities constitute almost all the social organization on the planet. The various sectors are parts of communities, as are the networks and informal relations that always exist. Hybrids like plantations or military bases can be handled as such, while monasteries, convents, and many military units do not qualify. That leaves the international organization that is still forming.

The postulate that each level of community may be a locus of causality implies comparisons of same-level communities (all counties, all towns, etc.) and interprets the health criterion as integral to community structure at each level. As Sampson and Wilson (1995:38-39) summarize the format: "The community level of explanation asks what it is about community structures and cultures that produces differential rates. . . ." They might have noted that Herbert Menzel (1950) suggested this strategy in response to an early article on the ecological fallacy. Accordingly, the version of social ecology presented here emphasizes the structural conceptualization and measurement of communities that comparative analysis requires. A structural dimension is systemic—spanning the whole system—and group-level, which means that it is defined by the constituent institutions of communities. Although in practice sectorial dimensions may enter the discussion, these are avoided as much as possible, as are aggregations of individual or household attributes.

Population Health

An empirical starting point is the acceptance of appropriate measures of population health as the criteria for assessing adaptive success. These rates across comparable communities range from self-reports to age-adjusted mortality to life expectancy. Ideally they are corrected for years lost because of disability. To judge by the rising demand for medical care, a long life free of disabilities is increasingly a world-wide aspiration and it is usually considered a "final good," not something that buys something else. Population health measures such as mortality rates can be disaggregated by age, sex, race, and administrative level, and are increasingly accurate for all levels of community over time and across regions. All these variants of population health contrast with reproductive superiority, the Darwinian criterion of evolutionary success. While it is true that some communities consciously strive for high rates of fertility, the residents of most countries have increasingly opted for fewer but healthier offspring. In the modern world, population health is a better measure of adaptive success. A further advantage of this criterion is that it shifts attention away from diseases and the biomedical model that explains these.

Threats

The neo-Darwinian model presented here pays special attention to existential threats such as resource depletion, corporate exploitation, the failure of a major production facility, an epidemic, or a large influx of a poor minority. These threats are constantly changing even after communities screen them to determine which are serious. Accordingly, they are summarized by a lower case letter "t". The introduction of this common-sense category is necessary for guiding the open-ended search for threats in a region and classifying them as "existential." At the local level, officials are the most convenient source of judgments as to the seriousness of a threat. The local media and government reports supplement these with evidence of pollution, deindustrialization, inter-community conflict, and the like. That phase sets the stage for the second step in the process, the construction of robust measures based on more objective data. A single criterion, such as the decline of the manu-facturing labor force or the loss of status by the white population is rare.

Transaction Organizations

When faced with problems such as the decline of a local industry, communities call on a wide range of "transaction organizations" in order to "solve" the problem. These are the problem-solving organizations that all communities depend upon. The list includes the familiar organizations that locate in and around communities: factories, firms, agencies, services, facilities, and the like that apply the "solutions" that communities have arrived at in the past. When new problems appear, communities review their repertoires and deploy an agency, expecting it to manage the problem. If an appropriate organization does not exist, communities borrow or create new agencies to deal with the challenge. Organizational responses are constantly changing in response to the shifting threats in the environment. Consequently, sociology cannot make universal statements about these threat-agency interactions. All that is possible are empirical generalizations and the calculations of efficiency that disciplines like economics offer.

But is it not true that transaction organizations can damage the biological and physical environment, sometimes beyond repair? Such impacts can hardly be denied, particularly when the damage reacts back on the community and becomes a threat, as happens at toxic waste sites almost everywhere. Such secondary threats are increasingly frequent around the world, and they have spawned "environmental agencies" that attempt to plan ahead to forestall them. And, of course, these protective agencies may cause further problems down the line, such as higher costs of housing and the marginalization of poor families.

Problem-Solving Capacity

The list of transaction organizations is endless and is constantly changing in response to changes in the environment. Consequently, the common-sense idea (ph=o), where ph is an indicator of population health appropriate to the community level under study and o is one or more health-related transaction organizations, is usually untestable. Only a few regions and their organizations are stable enough to permit such tests. Measurement is always problematic because the choice of items for an index is based on empirical knowledge and not on the more rigorous guidance of a concept. Given this inherent unreliability of transaction organization measures, as well as of their changing shape, this type of problem-solving capacity rarely produces strong correlations with measures of population health. Indeed, the correlations with medical facilities are often positive, an embarrassing and puzzling finding. (See Young, 2001, for an explanation.)

Should we conclude, then, that social ecological research using the population health criterion is fruitless? At this point, structural ecology invokes a strong remedy: It proposes three master adaptive strategies that exist to some degree in all communities. These strategies are differentiation (i.e., the division of labor) that generates specialized knowledge for problem-solving efforts; structural pluralism and the open debates over policy directions that some communities foster; and, last, mobilization behind a leader or a program in an effort to look at the problem from a different point of view. The three dimensions of capacity are intrinsic to human language and probably appeared with it, bestowing a powerful adaptive advantage on human communities.

The Durkheimian antecedents of the principal dimension of problem-solving capacity, structural differentiation, are easily recognizable, as is one source of solidarity/social movements for those who are familiar with Durkheim's book on religion. Structural pluralism or "contestation" derives from political science, especially the work of V. O. Key, Jr. (1951) on southern U.S. politics, and similar studies of democracy. What is new in the current usage is their interpretation as master adaptation strategies. Community leaders may not understand this classical theory, but everyone can understand problem-solving by means of specialized knowledge, weighing the alternatives for action and getting behind a reform movement.

The three structural dimensions form "profiles," posing the question of their differential impact. This is as yet uncharted territory, but the primacy of differentiation (i.e., socioeconomic status at the household level, urbanization at the provincial level, etc.) is plausible and is taken as a given by most social ecologists. Complementing it is structural pluralism, which is a component of the democratic form of government that is spreading, albeit haltingly, through all levels of community. By contrast, the many social movements that reflect community solidarity at different levels have not found an institutionalized form. It may be, however, that we are seeing the beginnings of this process in the proliferation of ethnic and other identity groups around the world.

This discussion of community problem-solving will strike some readers as misguided, because everyone knows that it takes individual minds to solve problems. But that criticism simply reflects the pervasive methodological individualism for which there is no answer other than to show how methodological structuralism is superior for solving sociological problems. Meanwhile, structural ecology makes a place for individuals as the lowest level of community because the threat/Capacity ratio applies equally well to people. They possess specialized knowledge and skills (that a vocabulary test will measure), varying degrees of the role-playing competence that facilitates contestation, and they are capable of constructing a one-person "social movement" that we call a career or even charisma. Like communities, their responses to challenges depend on their problem-solving capacity.

The Intervening Process

The formula $ph=C/t$ brings the principal terms together but it omits the intervening mechanisms that connect cause and effect. In the structural (as opposed to the reductionist) explanation proposed here, the intervening—"collective stress"— process is systemic, affecting all the members of the community in the same way, as happens when a community is under attack or when a community is forced to relocate. This condition that communities may experience is often called disorganization or disorder, but these terms obscure the group-level character of the process where individual responses are part of an emergent property. This type of structural (also holistic) causation has been noted by Diez-Roux (1998), who draws on Bunge's (2009:19) definition: "The behavior of an individual is determined by the over-all structure of the collection to which it belongs." Seeman and McEwen (1996) have reviewed the physiological processes that are involved.

Antecedents and Comparisons

Given the radical commitment of structural ecology to the community as the primary adaptive unit, we can put aside the many varieties of "human ecology" that focus on the individual, usually in an economic context. For these paradigms, community institutions function as a bundle of constraints and incentives. Insofar as institutions change in response to environmental pressures, they are recast as economic, on the basis of which the individual's choices shift. At the same time, aggregations of individual preferences shape the institutions of society. The perspective is broadly Weberian, a sociological perspective that is congenial to economic linkages.

Research in the Hawley (1950) ecology tradition makes the materialist assumption that social changes can only be explained by technology and the organization of production. Hawley (1984) has compared his model to Marxism and it is clear that many ecologists are materialists without being Marxist. But it is hard to see how a sectorial process can account for the systemic adaptation of communities. In addition, the central role of technology in materialist theories begs the question. That, after all, is one of the adaptive innovations that a theory is supposed to explain.

Structural ecology also parts company with encyclopedic schemes, such as the one Lenski (2005) has summarized in his capstone book. His model is oriented to the ecological-evolutionary changes in human social organization over the course of history and prehistory, while structural ecology looks at the contemporary dynamics. That is not a fundamental difference but the contrast of the two perspectives is still marked. As criteria of success, for example, Lenski lists production and consumption of goods; wealth and income; occupational and organizational specialization; inequalities of power, prestige and privilege; size of territories; and possession of mineral resources (2005:20). Energy consumption is a comprehensive criterion. As determinants of these criteria, Lenski lists the following: (1) "Humanity's common genetic heritage; (2) the various technologies that our species has fashioned to enhance this heritage; (3) the resources and constraints of the bio-physical environment; (4) the resources and constraints of the sociocultural environment; and (5) the impact of the process of intersocietal selection" (p. 7). These five categories are found in his introduction, where we should not expect specificity. But they are radically inclusive, whereas structural ecology excludes them.

The version of sociological ecology with which "structural ecology," as used here, aligns more closely is the loose paradigm known as the "Chicago School" (Park, 1952 [1936]). The similarity is captured by the dark prediction that "there goes the neighborhood," the title of the Wilson and Taub book mentioned in the introduction. This perspective is not constrained by the materialist assumption that the conditions of making a living determine social change; and the early researchers were more open to the many conflicts that existed within a generally peaceful city. They were also convinced that communities were adaptive units that need not be disaggregated into rational actors. Yet the overall similarities between Chicago social ecology and that presented here are overshadowed by differences, as a list of structural ecology's main features will demonstrate: a) the model accepts the consensus-based criterion of population health for evaluating community performance; b) it applies to all social groups that fit a (very broad) definition of community; c) it applies to a wide range of threats and community responses; d) its central concept is problem-solving capacity as reflected in three universal strategies; e) it makes a place for the programs and agencies (i.e., transaction organizations) that communities borrow or create to deal with known problems; f) it specifies the condition (strong and weak structural profiles) that determines the rise or decline of population health. More generally, structural ecology elaborates the cultural strand of Park's (1952: 156-7) exposition of human ecology.

Historical studies such as Diamond's *Guns, Germs and Steel* (1997) focus on the nation-state or its military arm as the unit of adaptation in versions of ecology that implicitly transpose the Darwinian triad of variation, selection, and reproductive superiority. As the title suggests, the book combines the biological version (germs that kill off the human enemy and allow population expansion into the depopulated territory) and a social version that turns on advantages in military technology and subsequent intermarriage with the enemy's women. Environmental "selection" takes the form of threats and problems that communities face, everything from epidemics to marauding armies.

The Plausibility of the Threat-Capacity Dynamic

The first question that most people ask about a new theory is: What is the evidence for it? That is probably not the best question to ask because consistency, comprehensiveness, and falsifiability are prior considerations. In the present context, we must take these features as given, and note that in the social sciences even a preliminary answer to the confirmation question may require decades. Realistically, all that can be expected at this point is plausibility, which can be established in three ways. But prior to these, it is usually possible to find illustrations of the process in the form of descriptions of relevant events or natural experiments. The Wilson and Taub (2006) interpretation of their ethnographic study that introduced this essay is an example. Another has appeared in the *Chronicle of Higher Education* and concerns the forced resignation of Lawrence Summers, a former president of Harvard. Bennis and Movius (2006) dismiss the many interpretations that turn on

Summers' perceived arrogance and the willfulness of faculty members. They argue, instead, that the acceleration of science and technology in modern universities has moved the center of gravity of elite universities from the humanities to the science–based applied disciplines. The effect of this rapid development at Harvard was to threaten to dethrone the humanities from their central role as the source and repository of knowledge about the human condition. The impending loss of status is exemplified by the rise of a new campus across the Charles River from the historic center of the university, and the humanities faculties reacted with an aggressive defense of the traditional core of the university. But their response reflected weakness as compared to the applied fields in the new campus, with their science-based and grant-rich laboratories, mathematical analysis, and international organization. Unfortunately, we have no information on the population health of the faculty.

Subsuming another Paradigm

A general strategy for establishing plausibility is to reinterpret a recognized body of research. Given the extension of the definition of community to the individuals, the research on "stressors" may be taken as an example. Thoits (1994; 2010) has summarized this paradigm by anchoring it in Selye's (1956) book *The Stress of Life* that stimulated a train of studies of "life events" such as serious accidents, a death of significant other, the loss of a job or a business, and the like, which can be classified as acute, chronic, or catastrophic (Turner, Lloyd and Wheaton 1995). These "stressors" were tested as potential causes of mental health problems with positive results, and the "buffering" role of social support was recognized early on. Protocols for measuring "coping," self-esteem, and "mastery" were introduced, and the responses to buffered events were rated as successful or unsuccessful. Wheaton (1985) codified the models that had been proposed and identified two, moderating and suppressing, as appropriate for the paradigm.

The similarities of the stress-buffering-adaptation model with the threat-capacity-adaptation sequence of social ecology are evident but there are some divergences. The stress model is limited to individuals although, from time to time, the term is used to characterize discrimination against a minority group. The ecology model starts and ends with groups, redefining individuals as groups, at least with respect to threat, capacity, and health. Measurement is also different. The several indexes for buffering show progress in measurement but they also reveal the absence of a clear concept. "Coping" is rather open-ended. By contrast, the social ecology concept of capacity identifies three primordial problem-solving strategies that provide more guidance in choosing indicators than do ordinary language words like "coping," "mastery," and "self-esteem." With regard to threats, the psychological model relies on interviews and observations for compiling a list while social ecology depends on community leaders to define threats. In practice, however, there is not much difference in the approaches, although the idea of threat introduces a focus that is lacking in the term "life events," even when those are selected as "undesirable."

A Better Explanation for a Known Relationship

A recent special issue of the premier *Journal of Health and Social Behavior* featured the "fundamental cause" explanation of the correlation between socioeconomic status and health (Phelan, Link and Tehranifar 2010). This explanation, which turns on the "resources" that high status people and households use to maintain their health, first appeared in 1995, and has quickly risen to the top of the list of four or five proposed explanations. These are reviewed in articles by Bunker, Gomby and Kehrer (1989), Cutler and Lleras-Muney (2008), and Young (2009).

A central insight is contained in the label that its authors have given to their proposed explanation. At first glance, "fundamental cause theory" smacks of public relations, but the phrase has a serious purpose in dramatizing a shift from the behavioral risks to the social factors that determine these. In effect, Link and Phelan (1995) reject the disease-mortality version of the biomedical explanation in favor of the more distal social causes. Of course, diseases still figure in this explanation as a changing intervening mechanism, so the biomedical model still operates.

Although Phelan et al. never labeled it as such, their analysis of the many risk factors and diseases that have changed over the years, while the basic socioeconomic status (SES)-health relationship remained stable, is one of a number of key features of the correlation that must be explained. Their contribution may be called the "alternative mechanism effect." The other features are: the invulnerability of the correlation, even when a wide range of control variables are included in the analysis; the gradient (i.e., stair step) effect when rates of ill health are graphed against each additional year of schooling; the "broad spectrum effect," whereby SES can be shown to reduce a large number of different diseases; the "life course effect," i.e., the fact that the correlation holds for all ages; the widening gap between the health of high and low SES people; and the "intensification effect" that shows up when the impact of a disease, such as tuberculosis, is worse for low status people. (See Young 2009:42ff for a detailed review with references.)

Some of these findings defy conventional wisdom. For example, a common explanation for the SES effect is that poor people live in dangerous neighborhoods, they smoke, they eat too much fat, they rarely see a doctor, and they have more health problems and disabilities to begin with. But when all of these factors are controlled statistically, the effects of number of years in school and income is still strong (Young, 2004). The gradient effect is equally surprising. In surveys of thousands of people across the United States, the wide variation in the kind and quality of schooling does not affect the basic pattern. On the evidence so far, simply sitting in a classroom for a year improves health over a lifetime. The broad spectrum effect can be dramatized by imagining that a pharmaceutical company discovers a drug that will cure or at least ameliorate many different diseases. Such a wonder drug would even surpass penicillin, which loses its potency as viruses develop resistance to it. The SES effect does not degrade over time and may even strengthen.

Phelan, Link and Tehranifar (2010:S34) summarize resource theory succinctly with the statements that "a superior collection of resources held by higher SES individuals and the collectivities to which they belong allow those of higher SES to avoid disease and death in widely diverse circumstances. . . . At the same time, this long-term stability in the association between SES and health/mortality results from the amalgamation of effects across many specific processes and conditions. New knowledge and technology relating to innumerable diseases emerges constantly." This statement and the supporting text underlines the centrality of resources in this theory. SES, which is not defined other than operationally as schooling and income, becomes an umbrella concept for the five principal resources: knowledge, money, power, prestige, and "beneficial" social ties. Other resources may exist, but the model takes these as central. These work through the risk and protective factors to produce higher levels of health. This is a standard quasi-reductionist format for explanation in sociology, except that here the risk/protective factors, which are mostly diseases and medical technology, are assumed to change over time.

As is evident from the diagram and the texts of their articles, Link and Phelan believe that they have found the explanation for the powerful SES effect. But there are some problems. Knowledge and money, for example, are at least partially synonymous with education and income that Link and Phelan designate as basic indicators of SES. Prestige overlaps with occupational rankings that are often used along with schooling, income, and membership in clubs as basic indicators. "Social ties" are limited to those that are "beneficial," a modification that seems to beg the question. "Power" is an old favorite in sociology even though it is almost impossible to define. A second question is whether these five are independent or form a bundle. They seem to be the latter, although they may be deployed, like the arrows in a quiver, for specific targets. Who decides on the targets and the resources to be deployed?

But these are minor points compared with the more general criticism that the five categories are so abstract and open-ended that they undermine the testability of the theory. While it is true that research teams can often agree on empirical indicators, that is an ad hoc procedure in comparison with concept-guided indicators. One reason the argument seems plausible may be that the whole sequence uses commonsense terms that are superficially understandable. These conventional meanings obscure a second problem, which is that the causal sequence does not really explain what it is about SES that produces health. The term "resources" suggests instrumentality but we never get past the words.

By contrast, the problem-solving explanation is radically sociological, and the process of social problem-solving explains what it is about indicators such as schooling or occupational complexity that determines health, defined as optimal (for age and disabilities) physical and mental performance. The reason that years in school, wealth, performing in a complex occupation (such as the government jobs in the famous Whitehall study), and participating in community organizations are powerful predictors of health is that they all provide training in applying specialized knowledge, comparing policy options and mobilizing behind a course of action. Attending any kind of school for one year may or may not improve reading, writing, and arithmetic, but it almost always improves problem-solving capacity. On the playground, children quickly learn that most games have positions that require specialized skills and the play usually involves a lot of argumentation.

Leaders are recognized and teams are chosen. Much the same thing happens in families and in the wider community. Membership in voluntary organizations or churches involves learning about how to participate in such groups.

What are the intervening processes in this explanation? Successful social problem-solving moderates the many collective stress reactions that occur among community members and establish a community social equilibrium that optimizes the molar (whole system) functions of the body. Problem-solving also moderates the many risk factors operating in a community, but these are so close to disease and mortality that it is preferable to treat them as an elaboration of the biomedical model, where they explain no more than fifty percent of annual deaths (See McGinnis and Foege 1993 and the replication by Mokdad et al. 2004).

This theory explains the strong correlation between SES indicators by identifying the process (improved social problem-solving capacity of individuals and households) that the indicators embody. Comparable indicators of the master strategies can be found or constructed for communities. The broad spectrum effect is explained by the molar physiological optimization, which protects against many diseases. The life course effect is explained by the human memory for techniques and practices of successful problem-solving. The cumulative mutual reinforcement of problem-solving practices intensifies the impact. This accumulation of successful problem-solving capacity also explains the widening gap in health that separates low status from the high SES people. In short, the problem-solving explanation really explains and the explanation can be tested.

Applying the Theory to a New Problem

The U.S. has seen many political movements that diverge from the platforms of the two principal parties (Hofstadter 1965; Bell 2002), but the "Tea Party" movement stands out for its unyielding nativist ideology and its ability to influence elections. Rasmussen and Schoen (2010) classify it as an example of right-wing populism, while Skocpol and Williamson (2012) characterize it as a political reaction to the possibility that Democrats might reshape policies for the longer term. How would structural ecology conceptualize this and similar movements? The formula C/t allows change in two directions: capacity can become greater than threat or threat can exceed capacity. Moreover, the shifts can be short-term or long-term. If the latter, we have a community where the leaders, at least, come to believe that their community lacks the capacity to reverse its long decline. In that circumstance, the clerics and secular ideologues appeal to the community's past as a source of strength. This "nativist" reaction can be summarized as the belief (and associated practices) that a way of life in the past was superior to that in the present and should be reinstated. There is no comparable term for the first kind of shift, where capacity is stronger than threat, but the terms "nationalist" and "independence" at the nation-state level and "populist" at regional and local levels convey the core belief that an imagined future way of life is superior to that in the present and is worth the struggle to attain it. Nationalist movements typically formulate a constitution or other foundational document while nativists identify an existing one for their obsessive attention. Both nativism and nationalism are well-known in the political science literature (Bell 2002), while anthropologists have studied both nativist and "revitalization" movements among the American Indians (Linton 1958/1943; Wallace 1956).

In their survey of Tea Party beliefs and practices, Skocpol and Williamson describe their many nativist attributes without classifying them as such. They begin (p. 48ff) with the almost religious reverence that Tea Partiers have for the Constitution. Like the sacred books of other such movements, it is interpreted as providing the foundation for an ideal society. Therefore, it must be studied frequently and in detail. Yet they believe in citizen activism and are skeptical of experts. They read the fine print of bills that come up in Congress and are sticklers for literal interpretations. Other themes are small government, fiscal discipline, free-market capitalism, and individual responsibility, all of which hark back to an imagined early period in U.S. history. They are against government regulation, the separation of church and state, many types of immigration, and "handouts" to those who did not work to contribute to Social Security. According to Skocpol and Williamson, Tea Party members favor workers over freeloaders, whites over minority groups, and the older generation to "overly entitled young people." They fear societal decline and worry about the future of the United States if Obama succeeds in transforming America.

The structural ratio hypothesis points to capacity and threat. The articles in the Bell (2002) edited volume refer to the "dispossession" of status and cultural identity among businessmen, managers, the military, and other such groups, Although Bell was mainly concerned with a range of statuses, loss was ubiquitous. Not mentioned in a book originally compiled in the 1960s is the threat to whites of rising ethnic groups now armed with institutionalized rights. But that is a reasonable instantiation and lends itself to rough measurement using available data. The capacity "dimension" poses the problem of finding the right combination, but using the appropriate community is the key, because the three dimensions always occur within communities.

Discussion

This article has proposed a fundamental process of social ecology and has compressed it into the formula ph=C/t, where ph refers to a measure of population health appropriate to the level of community under study, C refers to a composite index that combines the three master problem-solving strategies (the application of specialized knowledge, contestation over the merits of policies, and mobilization for reform movements), in order to look at the problem from a different angle). The changing ratio of capacity to threat is the starting point of the causal sequence. The dynamic can be found in all communities when these are defined as multi-functional groups where the governing body is concerned with the welfare of members. It is labeled "fundamental" because for each community level the ratio is the starting point of the causal sequence. It assumes that no other variable or a combination of variables makes a significant contribution to the causal sequence, and that it cannot be "derailed" by other variables even though some of these may modify the effect.

Is this hypothesis really fundamental? One argument, of "the buck stops here" type, has already been offered. The structural hypothesis points to a type of qualitative event in the form of a shift in the C/t ratio as the initiating cause of the sequence. Such shifts are more plausible than a rise or fall of a single variable, such as income inequality or population growth, because they reflect a type of change that disrupts any longstanding adaptation to the environment. Deciding when a particular ratio level has become chronic is more difficult and may depend on the accumulation of comparative cases. In addition to a starting event that is strong enough to reject counter-arguments of the form "it (i.e., the effect) would have happened anyway," there is another sense in which it is fundamental: the three variables are not open to displacement or additions that might capture more of the structural dynamic. Like the Darwinian triad that accounts for reproductive superiority, the ph=C/t formula combines community capacity, identification of existential threats, and a universal criterion of success, which is more appropriate to communities than reproductive superiority. Other variables are assumed to have only a temporary modifying effect.

What would it take to "prove" this hypothesis? Measures must be devised for the three terms of the formula, and statistical analysis must show that the interaction ratio predicts when other competing variables are controlled in tests at all levels of community and in many different contexts. After that, the hypothesis must be shown to hold in multilevel statistical tests and in change over time sequences for a range of intervening mechanisms. These may require two or more decades to reach closure. Lacking such a research program, the present essay has sought to establish the plausibility of the hypothesis with illustrations and by showing that the hypothesis can subsume the major features of the stress-buffering-adaptation paradigm, it can explain the SES effect on health more adequately than competing theories, and it can explain new phenomena such as the rise of the "Tea Party" movement.

Addendum to the Proposed Social Ecology Law

The purpose of this addendum is to defend the proposed ecological theory against the objection that it does not qualify as a "law," which may be written as follows:

$$ph=C/t$$

where ph refers to an appropriate—for the community level under study—measure of population health, C refers to problem-solving capacity, and t refers to a serious threat to the community. Communities are defined as multifunctional groups with a concern for their members, and their "levels" range from the household on up to the nation-state. The measure of population health must be appropriate to each level because it is defined, consensually, as a measure that is molar (i.e., whole body) and in the form of a rate that is appropriate to the age and disability structure of the population. An example is age-adjusted mortality rates across counties.

Capacity is an appropriate combination of the application of specialized skills, open debate on policy options and, on occasion, reform movements. It is written in uppercase to reflect the theoretical basis of these master strategies of adaptation. A threat to communities, by contrast, is an event or process that the leaders of the community have defined as a serious threat.

The equal sign in the equation signifies "is caused by" as elaborated below. The causality interpretation reflects the theoretical side of the equation. It also has an empirical side if the formula is taken as a probabilistic statement that can be tested statistically. But the interest here is theoretical. Thus, the formula can be expanded verbally as follows: If C and t are of equal strength, population health will be "normal" for the communities under study. If C is greater than t, population health will be above normal, and if C is less than t, population health will be lower.

Assuming the formula is empirically validated, should we call it a law? We can evaluate it against the five criteria that Rosenberg and McShea (2008:45) have listed for deciding whether a statement is a law. These are:

1. Is the candidate a true universal conditional that makes no mention of specific places, times or things?

2. Is the candidate a contingent statement the denial of which is conceivable, as opposed to a definition or the consequence of definitions that cannot support causal relations?

3. If the candidate is true only because of a *ceteris paribus* statement, can we expect to narrow the range of its exceptions by empirical means?

4. Does the candidate support counter-factual conditional statements?

5. Do we have great confidence in the validity of the law after only a relatively small number of observations? (This may overlap with the above.)

The answer to the first question is affirmative because the law applies to all human communities. It conceptualizes individuals as a special case of community because, like them, individuals apply specialized knowledge and skills, they mentally debate alternatives and, on occasion, they will radically change their position on an issue. So defined, communities comprehend almost all social organization on the planet. The multifunctional criterion implies the community "contains" the social organization that is associated with institutional sectors as well as networks of people or groups. That leaves no more than 5 percent of social organization that is not covered. The emerging international organization has not yet crystallized well enough to call it a community, and some smaller places, like plantations, may have only limited functions.

The answer to the second question is also affirmative, because it is conceivable that the positive capacity/threat ratio is not correlated with above normal population health, thereby passing the falsifiability test.

It is assumed that the proposition will hold "other things being equal," and that these other things could in principle be specified. For example, the threat of a hurricane may not last long enough for the law to have an impact. Another possibility is that a given level of community, say counties, is so constrained or disrupted by the actions of the state in which it is located that the law cannot operate. There are probably many other variables like these that would need to be controlled, but that is standard practice in sociology.

On the question of whether the proposed law supports counter-factual conditionals, it is clear that such a proposition could easily be stated: If the capacity/threat ratio were negative, population health would be lower.

Does the law have the "ring of truth," such that only a few tests would convince us that it is true? We do not have any rigorous tests as yet but there are some observations that are suggestive. People who have shown "resilience" in the face of adversity are well-known and some-times publicly praised. Likewise, nation-states sometimes surprise their contemporaries by solving a threatening problem or at least managing an existential threat. Some examples clearly involve problem solving but the question is whether they are examples of problem-solving as defined here. The Greek general Themistocles is well known in history for his solution to the problem of how to defeat the larger Persian fleet. The same is true of Nelson facing the Spanish Armada. More locally, some politicians seem to be more talented at problem-solving than others. Roosevelt, for example, hit on the deficit spending solution (probably with the help of his economic advisors) for bringing the Depression to an end without a knowledge of Keynes's theory.

The other question that arises when a proposed law is considered is whether it is backed by a theory that explains why the law works. Not all laws have such theories and some theories do not generate laws. In the present case, the mediating link between the causal ratio and the population health rate is a postulated "collective stress." An unmanaged threat to a community is hypothesized to generate pervasive stress in the community and the stress, if it persists, undercuts the health of all or most of the population. Specific diseases or behaviors may or may not appear and/or be labeled the "actual" cause of death (smoking, diet/inactivity, alcohol, microbial agents, and on to vehicle and gunshot deaths and illegal drugs), but such causes account for only 50 percent of annual deaths (McGinnis and Foege 1993), so is there is room for a direct impact of collective stress.

When problem-solving capacity is greater than the impact of the threat, then stress is minimal and the community attains an above-normal level of health. The theory rejects a reductionist sequence from cause to individual level processes and back up to the health rates. Collective stress of the type that is generated by the threat of war, the uncontrolled spread of a lethal disease, or economic collapse is felt by individuals but causality works through the emergent property that is generated by the unmanaged threat.

A final point is how to answer the question that many sociologists raise: How can you have a law in sociology when the problems that the discipline deals with are so complex? The smart answer to this question, which is really not an answer, is that the purpose of the law is to simplify this complexity. But the deeper reply takes the form of another question: How do we know that social reality is so complex? Maybe it is really simple but we are too slow-witted or prejudiced to appreciate it.

"WHAT'S THE MATTER WITH KANSAS?"
A SOCIOLOGICAL ANSWER

Abstract: *Thomas Frank's book poses a question: Why do working people in Kansas vote for Republican candidates when supporting them is antithetical to their economic interests? This article analyzes the statistical evidence for such alleged deviant voting and finds support for his thesis, because the working class does vote Republican. It also supports his principal causal suggestion for this hypothesized "backlash," the decline in average county population. But both variables lack a supporting theory. A "structural ecological" explanation for both facts claims that the fear that whites experience as the white population shrinks causes the backlash reaction and the Republican vote that Frank describes. Statistical tests support the alternative explanation, and illustrate the difference between Frank's ethnography-based arguments and the approach that most sociologists use.*

From time to time, insightful journalists have noticed anomalous trends that pose questions of fact and theory for the social sciences. The title of Thomas Frank's book (2004), *What's the Matter with Kansas?,* is one of these, and he rephrases it to: Why do so many voters in Kansas support Republican candidates in apparent contradiction to their economic interests? This unexpected correlation puzzled Frank, because he sees the Democrats as the party of "workers, the poor and the victimized." The contradiction between material condition and conservative voting is even more pronounced when one sees, as Frank does, the US electorate moving in a conservative direction. Frank's short answer to his question is that these voters are caught up in a backlash. They are reacting negatively to what they see as an expanding welfare state, the rise of a secular cultural elite, and the legalization of what was once considered immoral. On the question of what is causing this backlash, he is less clear and echoes the speculations of other journalists. "If pressed for a sociological explanation, they will attribute the conflict that roils the state to a squabble between fundamentalists and mainline Protestants, or a fight between the ignorant and the educated" (2004:102).

Most sociologists have probably read this book with appreciation, because the Midwest populism that permeates it is widely espoused. Some are able to put this political bias aside, but it is difficult when there is no accepted sociological alternative. Where are the conceptual and data analysis tools that could help us to make sense out of this puzzle? At the very least we should be asking: "What's the matter with sociology?" This analysis argues that sociologists now have a lot more scientific resources than they may realize. On the data analysis side, we have a wealth of new data sets that are easily accessible online, and the available statistical techniques are more than adequate for handling problems like these. Such tools can take us a long way but, of course, there is nothing so useful as a good theory. The second section of this paper argues that a theory exists that is capable of addressing this problem. As applied here, it points to the shrinking white population that white people believe is associated with the loss of status.

A Sociological Commentary on Frank's Thesis

Frank's diagnosis of Kansas' problems is not based on statistics except insofar as they are mentioned incidentally in the books he references. He relies mainly on unstructured interviews, newspaper articles, published speeches, and government reports—and the understanding that comes from having grown up in Kansas. His book does not attempt to separate facts from theory. That distinction is not part of his conceptual world and would not do justice to the book in any case, because it is a tightly interwoven exposition of a thesis that runs through the whole text. This journalist's report may be compared to the many ethnographies in anthropology that draw on the specialized knowledge and perspectives of "key informants" to weave a story line that integrates the book. Such "thematic ethnographies" continue to be written and some of them become (academic) bestsellers. But the analytic articles in professional journals have now become standard in the social sciences.

Accordingly, the first task is to identify the variables in the Kansas book, and it is evident that the Republican vote in national elections is the starting point. Frank is arguing that while most of these votes are traditional, in the sense that families have always voted that way, the total is inflated by the votes of people who do not understand their own interests. Fortunately, the measure of political orientation is a simple Republican-Democratic dichotomy. The proportion of Independents is miniscule. The key fact is that the proportion of the electorate that supported the Republican candidate in 2008 was 69 percent, increasing only slightly from the vote in 2000. This high percentage is at odds with the historical record that describes Kansas and other Midwestern states as strongly populist a century ago. Farmers organized "alliances" that helped them in their fight against the railroads, the grain middleman, and the tight money policies of the government (Postel, 2007). But as Wuthnow (2012:4) notes, the populist period was only a brief interlude from long-term conservatism.

The first predictor for Frank is poverty, because the poor may not vote their interests either (and the variable is needed as a control). The second variable is the "working class." This group is not precisely defined but it is bounded by the descriptions of other such occupational groups. Frank's vocabulary for these groups is rich and varied. He mentions the conservative ruling class, the CEO class, homegrown elites, white-collar types, upper-middle-class, the wealthy, unionized blue-collar workers, low-wage immigrant workers, and farmers, and most of his references include pithy adjectives. Many of these adjectives are mentioned in the context of an angry, dichotomous conflict: workers against upper middle class conservatives or against the dominant political leaders. This conflict permeates Frank's discussion of occupational groups, but it is still fair to say that he starts with an occupational framework that can be reproduced, to some extent, by assembling the relevant census categories.

Table 1 starts with the percent classified as officially poor (13 percent) in 2010. This measure is a census aggregate for the county population, and that fact must be kept in mind as we approach the question of causality. Table 1 also lists the proportion of full-time farmers and the combined percent of two blue collar census occupational categories, as detailed at the foot of the table. Regression analysis is used to determine the contribution each variable makes to the (statistical) explanation of Republican voting.

All of the predictors are statistically significant. The poor vote their Democratic interests and the farmers are traditionally conservative. The positive correlation for the blue collar category supports Frank's claim.
The data for these tables come from the County and City Data Book summary of the Census of Population unless otherwise noted.

Table 1 Regression analysis of Republican vote using occupational predictors

Predictors	PvoteR08
Ppoverty	-.40*
Pfarmers	.55*
Pbluecollar	.22*
R^2	.55

*Indicates a significance level of .05 or better.

PvoteR08=percent voting Republican, 2008. (69; 29-84; mean; minimum-maximum).
Ppoverty = percent families in poverty in 2010 according to the official criterion (13; 7-24).
Pfarmers = percent work force classified as farmers, 2007 (49; 32 - 66).
Pbluecollar = percent of labor force (29;12 - 46) classified as dealing with natural resources, construction, mainten-ance, production, transportation and material moving. Downloaded from the 2010 census via American Fact finder.

As important as they are to Frank's exposition, there is a great deal more to his argument than the interests of occupational groups. His claim that the working people are responding to cultural issues implies a more complex process. At times Frank sounds as if he believes that the corporate class is surreptitiously manipulating the workers. At one point, he remarks:

Here, after all, is a rebellion against the "establishment" that has wound up cutting the tax on inherited estates. Here is a movement whose response to the power structure is to make the rich even richer; whose answer to the inexorable degradation of working class life is to lash out angrily at labor unions and liberal workplace-safety programs; whose solution to the rise of ignorance in America is to pull the rug out from under public education. (2004:7)

But his proximate cause is voter backlash, which he describes as a working-class cultural movement militantly opposed to what it considers to be the excesses of the Sixties and thereafter. It is against abortion, affirmative action, and all attempts to separate church and state. It strives to dismantle the welfare state and "big government" so that Americans will be free again. It is against high taxes and borrowing that increases the national debt. In fact, "backlashers" are convinced that the rich and the powerful, along with the liberal media, atheistic scientists, and the Eastern elite are engaged in countless conspiracies against them. These believers are caught up in currents of religious fundamentalism, anti-government hostility, anti-intellectualism, anti-evolutionism, anti-safety- net legislation, and anti-immigration. All these are aspects of a syndrome that Frank clearly believes is pathological and spreading. The term "cultural" does not convey the ideological heat that Frank sees.

Can sociology analyze this complex ideology? In the only academic study of Frank's claims that has appeared so far, Bartels (2006:214) addresses the question of whether workers across the US have been influenced in their voting by six non-economic issues: abortion, women's role, affirmative action, government spending on services, government jobs, and defense spending. Following Frank's (revised) position with respect to indicators of class, Bartels divides the large National Election Studies sample into those with and without a college degree. Then he shows that the college voters attach more weight to these issues than the high school-only working class. On this evidence, Frank's impressions appear to be unfounded.

Moving beyond occupational interests and issues, Frank points to external threats like depopulation, the rise of the food trust, and the general reorganization of life in favor of the wealthy as possible causes. (2004:68). Table 2 shows a test of this type of predictor, starting with a control on income inequality corresponding to Frank's speculations about the wealthy. This measure predicts the Republican vote negatively (i.e., Democratic), contrary to hypothesis. Still, the descriptive statistics at the foot of the table show the gap between the rich and the poor in Kansas is not great.

In addition to inequality, two measures of economic change, the increase in the proportion of farmers and in the number of business establishments during the first decade were included as consistent with Frank's perspective. But these are nonsignificant, which is surprising because similar measures of change predicted the frequency of militias in 300 U.S. counties in the study by Van Dyke and Soule (2002). Only the measure of population change clearly predicts, negatively, supporting Frank's suggestion. Thus the greater the population increase in 2000-2010, the lower the proportion of Republican voters and, of course, the reverse is true, i.e., a decrease in population is associated with higher Republican voting. Frank does no more than mention this variable, and we do not know why he thinks it is causal. That is not part of his rhetorical strategy.

Table 2 Regression analysis of Republican vote using change predictors

Predictors	PvoteR08
Gini	-.17*
Ppop0010	-.53*
Pfarmers0207	-.03
Pestab0208	.04
R^2	.30

*Indicates significance level .05 or better. Source: US Census.
PvoteR08=percent voting Republican, 2008. (69; 29-84; mean; minimum-maximum).
Gini = Gini coefficient of income inequality, 2007. (.42; .34-.49)
Ppop0010 = percent population change 2000-2010 (-4; -22-23).
Pfarmers0207 = percent increase in proportion of farmers, 2002-2007   (-16; -31--7).
Pestab0208 = percent increase in number of establishments (manufacturing, retail, professional, and health), 2002-2008 (.03; -23-+26).

Summing up, the application of tested measures and multivariate statistical analysis sharpen some of Frank's ideas and provide stronger evidence in favor of his working-class conservative voting hypothesis. It also elaborates his brief mention of possible causes, supporting his suggestion of an association of population decline and Republican voting but rejecting related variables. The following section will illustrate the benefit of linking his backlash insight to the sociological literature. Despite these advantages, some will argue that sociological analysis does not add much to Frank's conclusions. It requires a great deal of time in finding data, checking measures, and comparing interpretations. That is true, but such concerns and self-corrections are intrinsic to the scientific method. The ethnography-based argument in Frank's book, where the analysis is necessarily confined to the recesses of his own mind, limits this type of transparency.

A Sociological Hypothesis

Frank was more interested in calling attention to the unexpected correlation between workers and the Republican vote than he was in explaining it. His interest in the correlation was political, and the blue-collar Republican vote was simply the anchor item in the whole cluster of beliefs and practices. He called this intercorrelated cluster a backlash but that term is not specific. The term "nativist" is preferable for this type of syndrome, because its more abstract definition implies that a better way of living existed in the past that should be maintained in the present. So construed, nativism has a long history in sociology and political science and it is still with us today.

The concept of nativism has roots in the periodic hostility in American history in response to surges of immigration. Lipset and Raab (1978/1970:15) echo this literature when they propose that right-wing radicalism appears in "those groups already possessing status who feel that the rapid social change threatens their own claims to high social positions, or enables previously lower status groups to claim equal status with their own." Linton's essay "Nativistic Movements" (1958/1943) may be taken as the starting point of anthropological attempts to understand this phenomenon. As summarized in Linton's article, anthropologists have focused on the many cults that have appeared in response to near-genocidal attacks by the U.S. He noted that "nativistic tendencies will be strongest in those classes or individuals who occupy a favored position and who feel this position threatened by culture change" (1958/1943:470). Van Dyke and Soule (2002) focus on the way mobilization of such reactive groups "occurs in response to threats produced by structural social changes," including "population shifts, economic restructuring, and the increasing political power of previously disenfranchised groups, such as African Americans, women, and Jews" (2002:497). The theoretical thread that draws these ideas together is the response of a community faced with an unmanageable threat for which the only available defense is reaching back into the past.

An important variant of these threat hypotheses is the "white status loss" hypothesis (Kaufmann 2004; Schrag 2010; Swain 2002; Walters 2003) and the "impending minority status" of the white population in the US. In his most recent "decline of the West" book, Patrick Buchanan (2012) devotes a whole chapter, entitled "The End of White America," to this topic. He starts his review with the dreaded year 2042 which, according to the US Census projection, will see the end of the white majority. This tipping point has already occurred in California where, according to Maharidge (1996), the many propositions that have been passed with overwhelming majorities are designed, at least in part, to limit or block the expanding Latino population. Following California's lead, other states have passed similar laws, sometimes using the identical language of the original. Although no survey data are available, there seems to be agreement among the journalistic accounts that whites are beginning to show widespread concern.

As it happens, an explanation of nativist ideology and its "nationalist" opposite (an imagined future way of life that is better than the present) is contained in a new version of the well-known social ecology that began at the University of Chicago in the 1920s. A recent example of this tradition is the Wilson and Taub (2006) book *There Goes the Neighborhood*, which examined the process of succession among the ethnic groups in Chicago's neighborhoods.

"Structural ecology" focuses on the characteristics of communities faced with similar existential threats, and hypothesizes that the level of problem-solving capacity determines whether they will react with nativism or nationalism. Problem-solving capacity is defined by three primordial strategies: the application of specialized knowledge, the institutionalization of public comparisons of policy and, in extreme cases, mobilization for reform. This last type of response is typically associated with a change in political or religious ideology. Thus, the fundamental cause of the backlash is the changing ratio of this composite "variable" relative to the intensity of the threat. If capacity is great relative to threat, the community will find a way to manage the inroads of, say, a new minority. If, on the other hand, capacity is weak and the ratio is negative, then a variant of nativist ideology will appear, fostered by local, mainly religious, intellectuals.

Given this core hypothesis of the theory (but see Young 2012 for more) one might ask where the measures of capacity are. One proxy is urbanization, which is a form of organization that often encompasses all three master adaptive strategies. Separate indicators for what may be called structural pluralism and reform movements are not yet available. Even so, the white status loss dynamic is congruent with the master Capacity/threat hypothesis and will serve as a test.

The comparison of voting means in Table 3 illustrates a simple format for testing the ratio interaction. The dichotomy of population size, above and below 30,000, is the proxy for urbanization (there are too few metro counties), which is interpreted as an indicator of problem-solving capacity. Within these categories, loss and gain in total population and for the white population are shown with their associated Republican votes. As Table 3 shows, the average loss and gain in total population predicts the Republican vote correctly (a 75 percent vote for the loss category and 70 percent for the gainers). In the high capacity urban category, the same gap (60 percent versus 55 percent) shows up, but at a lower level of Republican vote.

This positive finding for total population is a good start, but the ratio-interaction hypothesis favors white loss as the stronger predictor, because that is a more salient threat to the white population in Kansas. Accordingly, this comparison of means appears in the last columns of Table 3, which shows the Republican vote for the loss and gain categories of whites. These predict less strongly than total population, contrary to the ratio-interaction hypothesis.

Table 3 Comparison of means for Republican vote by urban status and percent loss-gain of white population

Rural-Urban	N	Ppop change	Repub. vote	N	Pwhite change	Repub. vote
Rural	46	1 loss	75	63	1 loss	73
	40	2 gain	70	25	2 gain	71
	86	Total	73	88	Total	72
Urban	2	1 loss	60	6	1 loss	59
	17	2 gain	55	11	2 gain	54
	19	Total	55	17	Total	58

Rural-Urban= a dichotomy, counties with 30,000 or more population are classified as Urban versus the rural counties with smaller populations. (1=82%, with a mean 8300; 1247-29180)(2=18% with a mean of 112590; 32787-544197) Pwhite change=pwhite0010, percent change in white population, as measured by (pwhite2010-pwhite2000). (-6; -32-6). Note: The formula used in this table for white change is a substitute for the standard measure based on the formula: pwhite0010=(white2010-white2000)/white2000). See text.

It is important to mention that growth (and decline) of the white population is measured in Table 3 by an alternative formula. The standard measure that was used for total population and, initially, for the white population (see the formula at the foot of the table) is undermined

158 Frank W. Young

by the negative correlation of white and total population change. Kansas has relatively few nonwhites, so total population and the number of non-whites are correlated .99. But the two standard measures of change are negatively correlated -.75. The explanation for this surprising fact is that total population growth includes nonwhites, so the proportion of whites decreases as total population grows. The alternative measure of white change avoids this problem.

Overall, these differences are not large but they fit the interaction hypothesis. Inasmuch as this table reflects the universe of Kansas' 105 counties, the absence of a significance test is not serious. Technically, tests of significance are not necessary when working with the universe, but most sociologists compute them as a guide to assessing the results (as in Tables 1 and 2). Further tests with larger samples and explicit measures of interaction (Hibbs 1973:47ff; Southwood 1978) should validate this initial finding.

A feature of the comparison of means format is that it illustrates a concept of causality that is rare in sociology. As reviewed by Van Dyke and Soule (2002) under the label "strain," it was discussed in the early sociological literature only to be dropped later on. But ignoring this type of causation, which captures the meaning of that term better than the shifts of a single variable, is a long-term mistake. A second feature, al-ready mentioned, is that the community—counties, in this study—is the locus of causality and the causal chain is community-specific. It does not drop down to the individual level, as does the standard reductionist for-mat. This non-reductionist sequence is consistent with the variables that are measured as community processes and the aggregates that are here construed as emergent properties.

Conclusion and Discussion

The research reported in this article explores Thomas Frank's (2004) thesis that the working people in Kansas have been supporting the Re-publican Party in recent years in opposition to their material interests. According to Frank, they do this because they are part of a conservative backlash that ranks traditional cultural values over economic interests. Meanwhile, their wages have stagnated and the rich have sharply in-creased their wealth. Much of the force of Frank's argument depends on his use of vivid and arresting word pictures and the rhetorical power of his materialist claim. By contrast, the counter-hypothesis presented here uses the combination of explicit theory and quantitative analysis that has now become standard among professional social scientists. The evidence generated by this analysis supports both Frank's working class conservatism claim and his hypothesis that decreasing population size contributes to the backlash syndrome.

An alternative hypothesis explains the increase in nativism, which includes the Republican vote, as a response to the white status loss that many communities are experiencing. When the social problem-solving capacities of these communities prove inadequate, local intellectuals formulate a nativistic path to a way of life remembered, with mythical elaborations, from the past. Communities that retreat along the nativist path are not irrational or victims of a corporate scam. Rather, they reach back to the past for a picture of the world that will guide their attempts to defend the integrity of their communities. Thus, the sociological answer to Frank's question "What's the matter with Kansas?" is that its communities are dealing as best they can with an inexorable process of demographic and cultural change, with all the status disadvantages associated with the loss of dominant white status. The many practices that express their defensive nativism are pathological in the usual meaning of that word, but such extreme mobilization may sometimes be the fever that helps cure the disease.

THE ISLAMIC COUNTER-REFORMATION

Abstract: *Radical Islamic groups are "nativistic" when they claim that a past way of life is superior to that of the present and should be imposed by any means possible. Such groups have become more militant since about 1980 and they have developed both national and international levels of organization. Comparable groups exist in the major religions and have targeted the U.S. more than other countries. All four of these facts must be explained. Revisiting the European Reformation and Counter-Reformation provides insights into the dynamics of this "global rebellion," and suggests that it is a reaction this time around to the existential threat embodied in the spreading human rights movement. The hypothesis that weak communities faced with an existential threat will respond with nativism explains this and other such movements.*

The surge in Islamic militancy is a recent development. A convenient starting point is the Iranian revolution of 1979 that installed a theocracy, and was followed by state takeovers and the imposition of sharia (religious) law in two other countries—Sudan and post-Soviet Afghanistan—and by armed threats to several others (Algeria, Somalia, Yemen). At least one Islamic group, in Turkey, has become a political party, and others are attempting to use democratic institutions to gain power. Still other Islamic groups are infiltrating key institutions, such as the army in Pakistan and the legal system in Britain (MacEoin, 2009). The controversy over head scarves and burkas continues. Subsequent paragraphs will offer a more precise definition of the contemporary Islamic militancy, but these indicators underline the need for a comprehensive explanation. The analytic strategy used here compares the current conflict to the Protestant-Catholic clash in the sixteenth century, drawing out a number of insights from that period and applying them to the present. In brief, we are seeing a rerun of the European Reformation-Counter-Reformation with the difference that this time the conflict is global. This claim implies that the two pairs of social movements are structurally congruent and can be explained by the same hypothesis.

Nationalist versus Nativist Movements

Starting about 1970, sociologists pursued an intensified interest in historical sociology, especially the anti-colonial independence movements after World War II. These new movements were "nationalist" in the sense that they aspired to create a new type of society that was thought to be better than that of the present. They typically drafted constitutions to guide their future course. By contrast, the Iranian revolution introduced an opposing movement, one that subscribed to the belief that a way of life in the past was superior to that in the present and should be imposed by force if necessary. These two types, nationalist and nativist (see also Farhang 1988) guide the classification of the European Reformation/Counter-Reformation conflict, because the first was nationalist in the broad sense used here and the counter-movement was nativist.

The classification of Islamic radicalism as nativistic turns on the attempts to impose sharia law in a target country. Sharia is a body of religious law that was codified about three centuries after Mohammed and has since been adapted to new circumstances (MacEoin 2009:1). It is totalistic in controlling almost all behaviors, private and public, and it still contains restrictions on women and harsh punishments for some crimes. Saudi Arabia seems to be extreme in its application of sharia, although cases of stoning and amputation are in fact rare (Feldman 2008:48).

The recent surge in Islamic militancy is also reflected in the rapid spread of the Muslim Brotherhoods. This "social movement organization" originated in Egypt in 1928 and now has branches in fifteen countries including the U.S., the U.K. and Israel, with links to Asia (Kepel 2004:171ff). The Brotherhoods claim to be peaceful but they have been associated with violence and, in some countries, they urge Islamists to form a state within a state (Farhang 1988).

Another way to assess the spread of Islamic militancy is to identify the cluster of "ideal type" attributes (also called a "range definition"), a method that Max Weber famously introduced in defining "bureaucracy." The list begins with sharia law as the defining feature. The second item is almost coterminous with the first, because after "successful attacks" on weak governments the imposition of sharia law invariably follows. A third item is the appeal to the Koran and similar sacred books as the source of unassailable truth, one precept of which is that Islam tolerates other religions only as second-class faiths. Male dominance and patriarchy are strong and there is little protection for women. Extreme violence and any stratagem may be used against apostates and infidels. The merging of church and state is omitted from this list because it is often ambiguous and, therefore, unreliable. These items are drawn from the literature and constitute a "measurement hypothesis" that has yet to be tested, by showing the inter-correlation of these items across a sample of Muslim countries. Further research should turn up other indicators and the statistical (e.g., factor) analysis may require some to be dropped.

When the indicators of Islamic nativism are generalized, it is apparent that similar nativist movements can be found for Judaism and Christianity. Juergensmeyer (2008) has summarized these contemporary nativist movements with the term "global rebellion," and he notes that they are all intent on rejecting the secular state. Nativism based on a return to Maoism has appeared in Peru ("Shining Path"), eastern India, and in Nepal, where it has captured a near majority of seats in parliament. This fact, of nativism arising in the context of several religions and ideologies, dramatically enlarges the task of explanation. Now, in addition to explaining the surge in Islamic militancy over the last thirty years, we must explain the similar militancy in different cultural contexts. This challenge increases the difficulty of finding a common cause but it also calls into question explanations that apply only to Islam.

Islamic nativism has developed several levels of organization: Al Qaeda at the international level, Taliban-type movements for state take-overs, and self-generated cells of like-minded young men in many countries. The Taliban type is more numerous and has stable features that facilitate comparisons. It is, therefore, the more manageable target for explanation. This and the other two levels of organization constitute the "nativist" problem of the twenty-first century. A comparison with the Reformation-Counter-Reformation conflict in sixteenth-century Europe offers a useful perspective, despite the five-century interval.

The Protestant Reformation and the Catholic Counter-Reformation

A range definition for the Catholic Counter-Reformation of the sixteenth century begins with the reaffirmation of the structure and beliefs of the medieval church. Searle's (1974:93ff) summary of the decisions of the Council of Trent (three sessions during the years 1545-1563) emphasizes this return to medieval orthodoxy. Specifically, Trent confirmed purgatory, indulgences, celibacy, veneration of saints, Christ's body sacrificed anew during each mass; seminaries for priests; bishops' authority from Pope, not God; tighter discipline; prohibition of academic studies of the Bible; no participation of laity in decisions; Pope's authority supreme; and the rule that people could find God only through the Church. The scope of the Index, excommunication, and the Inquisition was enlarged. Note that the Catholic Counter-Reformation did not attempt to return to the primitive Christian church. There have been such groups (reflected in the vows of poverty of some orders), and they illustrate the way versions of nativism develop in different contexts and at all levels of community: nation-state, provinces, villages, and even households.

Juxtaposing the two social movements and calling one a "counter-reformation," as the German historian von Ranke did, implies an action-reaction dynamic that is probably too simple. Even when the Reformation is judged to be an existential threat to Catholic orthodoxy, some countries (Poland, France) produced a counter-movement that was strong enough to reject it. An additional variable of organizational strength or weakness must be recognized. This third dimension is embodied in the pervasive hierarchy and the feudalistic economy that burdened Catholicism in southern Europe versus the increasing strength of the towns and principalities in northern Europe.

Identifying the Contemporary Equivalent to the Protestant Movement

What then is "Reformation II," as the contemporary existential threat to Islam and the other religions may be called? The claim here is that the formulation and acceptance by the United Nations of the Universal Declaration of Human Rights (UDHR) is the existential threat that provokes Islamic nativism. This document was completed by an international committee under the chairmanship of Eleanor Roosevelt, and presented in 1948, after which it catalyzed a social movement that has spread around the globe (Morgan 2010). Of course, there had been many rights documents, going back to the Magna Carta, but they were mainly concerned with the defense of citizens against tyrannical governments. The 1948 document contained such citizen rights and its thirty clusters listed many new positive rights (Levin 1996:21ff). More specifically these are:

The right to life, liberty, and security of person; freedom from slavery and torture; equality before the law; protection against arbitrary arrest, detention or exile; the right to a fair trial; the right to own property; political participation; the right to marriage; the fundamental freedoms of thought, conscience and religion, opinion and expression; freedom of peaceful assembly and association; and the right to take part in the government of his/her country, directly or through freely chosen representatives.

The second category includes economic, social, and cultural rights, which relate to, amongst others: "the right to work; equal pay for equal work; the right to form and join trade unions; the right to an adequate standard of living; the right to education; and the right to participate freely in cultural life."

The Declaration is more than an idealistic document because its clauses can be and have been incorporated in more than eighty universal and regional conventions that have the force of international law. The list of protected rights has been steadily enlarged and focused since 1991 (Levin 1996:57ff), and the rights momentum accelerated in 1993 when the Vienna Declaration and Programme of Action declared human rights an international responsibility that individual states were expected to support. Since then, people all over the world have become conscious of rights, and "rights talk" can be heard in remote corners of the globe. People now demand the right to have rights and in repressive states many of those who have attempted to exercise rights have been imprisoned and executed for doing so.

The conclusion of Tibi's (2002) survey is that human rights are the basis of a new moral order adapted to modern times. Their force and coherence are reinforced by the popular support of educated people around the world. This is not a clash of civilizations because, under normal conditions, civilizations can co-exist. Rather, it is a clash between a strong Western social movement, comparable to the European Reformation, and the threatened populations of a number of civilizations, including fundamentalist Christians in the West. Mayer's (1999) review of the conflict reveals a frequent tactic that reflects its force: Some human rights, especially those concerned with women's status and the exercise of religion, are antithetical to Islamic law, but only a few governments actually say as much. Such is the prestige of UDHR around the world, that governments claim to accept them—with the proviso that Islamic law may overrule secular rights. In other cases, summaries of Islamic law are made to sound like human rights until the reader realizes that crucial rights are omitted from the list.

The rights movement is a threat to all traditional societies, especially when the universal rights are incorporated into law. It is a social movement that impinges relentlessly, pervasively, and insidiously on traditional organizations. Islamists target America because that is where the UDHR originated and has been most strongly championed. President Carter made it the centerpiece of his foreign policy in 1977, and monitoring agencies, like Human Rights Watch and Amnesty International, are based in the U.S. If we allow for the typically slow initial stage of the movement (Morgan 2010), then its spread correlates with the intensification of Islamic militancy and similar eruptions around the world.

Explaining Nativist Militancy

Many explanations have been proposed for the current militancy: the impact of modernization; "jealousy of American freedoms and way of life;" the historical decline and humiliation of the followers of Islam, beginning with the Ottoman failure to capture Vienna in 1683; corrupt and autocratic governments; the mass media diffusion of the excesses of the "Sixties;" and "blowback" from U.S. proxy wars. There are a number of empirical objections to some or all of these hypothesized causes. Many of them do not account for the recent surge of nativism around the world. Some explanations, like "blowback," media excess, and jealousy, focus on the assumed American origin of these events, but their claims fail when it comes to the Maoists. Almost all of the proposed explanations have a large psychological component (i.e., anger, jealousy, resentment) without explaining how these individual traits are generated or how they produce the emergent property that the term "social movement" implies.

The most popular explanation, however, is that the Islamic world is simply defending itself against aggressive American policies (Nimer 2007). According to the CIA's early report (Scheuer 2004:11ff) on bin Laden's beliefs, as compiled from his own pronouncements, this "imperialism" has manifold components: The U.S. challenges God's word by declaring jihadists to be criminals; the U.S. supports oppression in

Kashmir, Philippines, Chechnya, the Chinese province of Xinjiang and in Palestine; the U.S. sends troops to the Philippines, Caucasus, Yemen, and Eastern Africa; the U.S. supports apostate Islamic governments in Kuwait, Egypt, Jordan, Saudi Arabia, and elsewhere; the U.S. occupies Iraq in order to control its oil; the U.S. helps the UN to separate Timor from Indonesia and set it up as a Christian state; U.S. occupation of Iraq, Afghanistan and the smaller states in the Gulf; the U.S.backing Israel's occupation of Muslim Palestine.

As vivid as the indictment is, it and the other proposed causes fail to address all aspects of the problem: Why now, why in all religions, why target the U.S., and why multi-level? At first glance, the "American policies" explanation seems to answer these questions. American power replaced British control in the Middle East after World War II; American influence is global, affecting religions everywhere; America has engaged in neocolonial interventions; and the defenses against American media requires both a coordinating executive and localized units. Nevertheless, "U.S. Policies" does not qualify as a causal explanation. Unlike the Reformation, "Policy" is too diffuse. It is like using a feather duster to drive a nail when a hammer is required. Scattered across countries and situations in many different forms, about the only unity that "U.S. Policy" has is the label.

A second problem with the Policies explanation is that it does not address the process by which the perception of pernicious policies is converted to the nativist ideology of retreat. With nativism, we are well beyond simple questions like "Why do they hate us?" because we are confronted with a social movement that can only be understood as a response to an all-encompassing threat. The many rural religious specialists around the world are aware of the human rights threat to their way of life, and in their weakness have formulated a return to the past, which they then propagate to unemployed youth, especially.

A third problem with Policies as cause is that it implies a simplistic explanation. It claims that a particular policy impinges on a region or a state, generates anger, and is automatically converted to religious hatred. Admittedly, the accounts of the Reformation-Counter-Reformation argue a similar process, and that "action-reaction" hypothesis is open to the same criticism. But other variables, those that regularly modify the impact of responses to threat, are surely involved. The one proposed here is "problem-solving capacity." This process of institutionalized problem-solving may be defined as the application of the three most frequent master strategies of adaptation: specialized knowledge, the public comparison of policy options, and, in extreme cases, mobilizing for reform (Young 2012). Faced with a serious threat, a community that is weak in problem-solving capacity will respond with a nativistic response.

The Vatican-directed Catholic domination of southern Europe in the sixteenth century embodies the kind of organizational weakness that the theory requires. As compared to the north of Europe, the south was organizationally rigid because of the Vatican's suppression of theological and philosophical thinking, the stagnation of economic innovation in the still-functioning feudal economy, and the suppression of dissent by the monarchies (Cameron 2006; Schilling 2008). Two other events that are usually overlooked are the contraction of economic activity that resulted from the cataclysmic population decline in the plague-ravaged fourteenth century (Cameron 2006:2) and the enforced migration of talented religious minorities. The Jewish Diaspora out of Spain strengthened the Netherlands and weakened the country of origin (Schilling 2008:39). About the only strong macro pattern in southern Europe was urbanization. According to Scott (2006:35) 17 percent of the population of Italy and Iberia were in towns of 5,000 or more inhabitants as compared with only 8 percent north of the Alps. But Scott undercuts even this key point by acknowledging that some of these cities grew "hyper-trophically," that is, the populations increased without corresponding urban organization.

Accordingly, we should expect to see that the governments of many Arab countries are weak and losing ground. The first UN-sponsored *Arab Human Development Report of 2003* (2005), written by Arab scholars, listed the many acknowledged deficiencies of the Arab states. For example, "On average, only 4.4 translated books per million people were published in the first five years of the 1980s . . . while the corresponding rate in Hungary was 519 books and in Spain 920 books" (2003 :4). All the other figures are equally dismal. Even their oil wealth has a down side because it must be managed by outside workers, and it gives the government power to dispense largesse without the scrutiny of taxpayers.

The rights movement is a threat to traditional societies because the international conventions are coherent and have the force of law. Whitaker (2009:176ff) lists seven such conventions that most of the twenty-one Middle East states in his list have only reluctantly signed. They are acutely aware of international pressure to sign the conventions, because they must defend themselves by claiming exemptions on the basis of Islamic law. In one case, at an international conference in Vienna in 1993, the Arab states formed a coalition that explicitly opposed the elevation of human rights to the status of an international morality (Tibi 2002:91).

The rights explanation can explain how a threat is converted to nativism. The crucial intervening process is the reaction of traditional religious specialists. Limited by their narrow view of the world (Nojumi 2008:106; Toth 2005:124) and convinced that their world is under attack, they have no alternative but to borrow or formulate a version of the faith that makes the past sacred. Actual data on the role of clerics does not yet exist, but we have an authoritative statement by the Ayatollah Khomeini: "What they call human rights is nothing but a collection of corrupt rules worked out by Zionists to destroy all true religions. . . . When we want to find out what is right and what is wrong, we do not go to the United Nations; we go to the Holy Koran. For us the Universal Declaration of Human Rights is nothing but a collection of mumbo-jumbo by disciples of Satan" (quoted in Mayer 1999:27). Along with their reaffirmation of the better world of the past, these ideologues seize on any complaint about the West that may offer a tactical advantage: neo-colonialism, godlessness, greed, conniving over oil, militaristic capitalism, to name a few, are all hurled at the West like stones in the intifada.

In sum, the rights movement stands as a focused existential threat to traditional societies around the world. It specifically contradicts the whole spirit of sharia law. As Mayer (1999) summarizes the situation: "To date one cannot point to a single government purporting to accord supremacy to Islamic law that has shown any real solicitude for protecting human rights as embodied in the local constitution, much less human rights as established in international law." Less serious, but nonetheless emblematic, are the many examples of the way governments effectively cancel the country's constitutional protections, by adding vague provisos requiring all laws to be based on Islamic criteria and giving the clerics the power to declare laws "un-Islamic."

Some Implications

The history of the European Reformation/Counter Reformation conflict suggests that the world is facing something similar and with it a long period of conflict. Europe finally reached a religious equilibrium in the course of a century or more (Mullett 1984:33), after which no more lands changed their religious adherence. Even assuming that the West continues to make progress in learning how to handle this problem militarily (Schmitt and Shanker 2011), we may expect a period of fifty years or more for the present conflict to subside.

Turning to the implications of the proposed "Capacity/Threat" hypothesis, we have two "variables" to work with. Can these be changed in ways that will reduce nativism? Can the threat be decreased and/or problem-solving capacity increased? The immediate problem is that the human rights threat to traditional societies is also a valued social movement in the West, and westerners are unlikely to give up the progress they have made. Most believe that it is the basis of a superior international legal system and should supersede the legacies of tribal societies. All such sweeping change has a down side and violent reactions are to be expected. In practice, many sharp edges can be smoothed over. There may be cases where the threat embodied in the rights movement can be reduced by negotiation or simply by ignoring the undercutting that Islamic countries are already practicing (See Little et al. 1998).

What about the other variable, capacity? That dimension is multifaceted and difficult to change even in advanced democracies. The challenge appears even with attempts to increase the major component of problem-solving—the differentiation of the division of labor. Perhaps, though, the task of increasing differentiation will solve itself. The spread of cities seems to be inexorable, and while some of these are simply clusters of tribal enclaves, they rapidly develop specialized knowledge. With modern communications and economic competition among countries, this process is accelerating.

The problem comes with pluralism which, although it takes many forms—from street marches to parliaments—is nonetheless fragile, especially in tribal societies. The same is true of political reform movements, such as the 2011 populist movement among Arab countries. We need a classification of traditional societies that guides the selection of potentially tractable cases. For example, the independent but still tribal states may be divided into those that recognize some rights for women versus those that do not. Countries like Afghanistan, Algeria, Iraq, and Indonesia are examples of the first type, while Somalia, Saudi Arabia, and Yemen limit such rights. The status of women is only one marker, of course, but it tends to divide countries with educated elites and secular governments from those where education is traditional and controlled by religious leaders. Once this distinction is made, the women's rights countries (and regions within countries) can perhaps be reached by persuasion.

QUALITATIVE SOCIOLOGY AS A NATIVISTIC MOVEMENT

Abstract: *The recent surge of articles and new journals that refer to "qualitative methods" reflects a nativistic intellectual movement. It shows the rapid expansion that is typical of social movements, along with neologisms, redefinitions, new textbooks, and antagonism toward the dominance of "quantitative methods" in sociology. Like other examples of nativism, it seeks to reinstate a past way of doing social research as superior to methods used in the present. The appearance of this movement in the latter part of the twentieth century can be explained as the adaptive response of a weak faction of the discipline faced with an existential threat, in this case, the dominance of "positivist, quantitative" methods. As such, it illustrates a central dynamic of a version of social ecology that defines weakness as inadequate problem-solving capacity. The application of this interaction hypothesis for reducing conflict is explored.*

Why are "quantitative sociologists" more willing to use qualitative methods and data, while "qualitative sociologists" resist almost all forms of quantification? The "positivists," as the first group has been called, use general interviews and even participant observation for gathering the information needed to construct formal instruments, such as household surveys. Then, when the results are in, qualitative data supply illustrations and sometimes examples of intervening mechanisms. The positivist attitude seems to be that qualitative methods are all right in their (auxiliary) place, but theory, instrumentation, and statistics are fundamental and define the core methodology of sociology. This generalization describing an asymmetric relationship between the two methodology factions is suggested by a number of summary statements. Guba (1985), for example, presents a sharp contrast between the "positivist" and "naturalist" programs and concludes that there is no room for compromise. Hall (2001:12613) sums up the antagonism in his encyclopedia article: "Contemporary qualitative inquiry is a product of critical and postmodern reactions to the research practices spawned of modernity." And Searle (2001:1363) notes: "There is, amongst this community, a popular 'creation myth' that typifies 'quantitative research' as a set of somewhat oppressive practices against which qualitative work emerged in heroic opposition."

This essay examines the "qualitative–quantitative asymmetry" by classifying qualitative sociology as an instance of a "nativistic" social movement that is based on the belief that a former way of doing research is superior to contemporary methods and should be reinstated. A "nationalistic" movement, by contrast, is based on the belief that a future way of doing research promises to be superior. Each type references "sacred" charter statements and strives to create new organizations and convert old ones in their drive for dominance. As it happens, the literature on social movements contains an embryonic explanation of the appearance of these two types of movements, and a revised version of the underlying theory will be applied to the task of explaining the remarkable rise of qualitative sociology since about 1970. The article proceeds by formulating an ideal type definition of "qualitative methods" and justifying it as "nativist." The application of the revised theory is illustrated with relevant facts but a comprehensive test is beyond the scope of this essay.

Qualitative Sociology as a Nativisitic Movement

The earmarks of a social movement, even one that is internal to an academic discipline, are well-known: a statement of goals that opposes the dominant policies; the florescence of a new vocabulary and practices; the appearance of one or more dedicated "social movement organizations;" and a rapid expansion that tends to follow a logistic curve: slow at the start, followed by a sharp, upward "bandwagon effect" and then a plateau.

Miles and Huberman (1994:1) describe the rise of this movement as follows:

> The expansion of qualitative inquiry since the first edition of this book (Miles & Huberman, 1984) has been phenomenal. The base of books, articles, and papers we collected for this second edition has more than tripled over that for the first. Debate on underlying epistemological issues has continued vigorously (Guba, 1985). There are full-fledged handbooks (Denzin & Lincoln, 1994; LeCompte, Millroy, & Preissle, 1992, Sage's Qualitative Research Methods series (more than 24 volumes), new journals (*Qualitative Studies in Education, Qualitative Health Research*), newsletters (*Cultural Anthropology Methods*), annual forums (Ethnography in Education

Research Forum; Qualitative Research in Education Conference), computer bulletin boards (QUIL.), software meetings
(International Conferences on Computers and Qualitative
Methodology), and special qualitative interest groups in most
major professional associations.

Figure 1 shows the cumulative increase of U.S. journals devoted to
qualitative sociology. The graph suggests that the surge was strongest
around 1990 and may now, as of 2010, be slowing to a plateau. The list
of journals used in the graph is probably not exhaustive but it illustrates
another diagnostic feature: They are all specialized for qualitative methods and topics. Articles using and discussing quantitative methods, by
contrast, simply appear in the general journals, many of which also
publish qualitative studies.

Figure 1 Cumulative Increase In Qualitative Methods Journals, 1970-2005

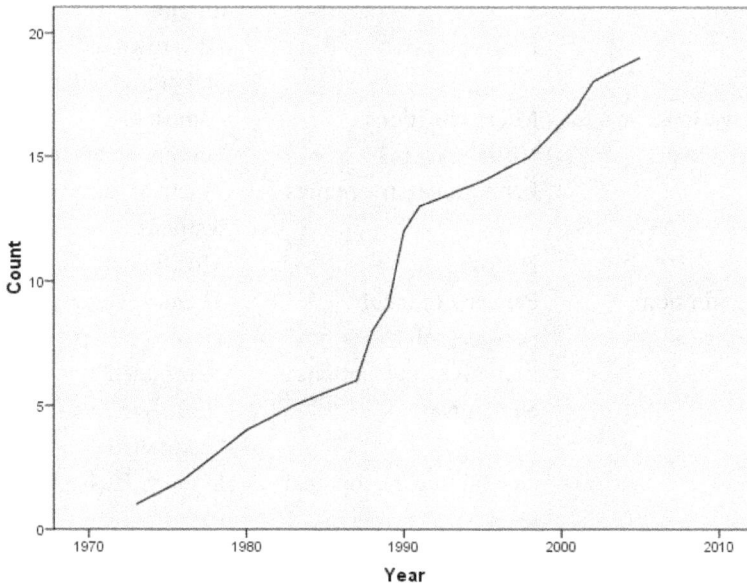

The diagnostic attributes of this movement may be listed with the
aim of defining an ideal type, one that captures the typical empirical indicators and allows for missing attributes. This mode of definition is
associated with the work of Max Weber, who used it to define "bureaucracy" and similar "formations" in economic history. But it is quite use-

ful for contemporary phenomena, and such empirical types can be rigorously defined and measured with factor analysis or a similar data reduction program. Table 1 lists the attributes that may be extracted from the many publications on qualitative methods. With the help of additional codification, they serve as a measurement hypothesis that awaits a rigorous test.

Table 1 Primary and secondary attributes of an ideal type definition of qualitative methods

Primary	Secondary	Examples and comments
Interviews, unstructured	Oral histories	
	Documents, expressive	Diaries, novels, editorials
	Documents, descriptive	Ethnographies, news articles
	Focus groups	Also town hall discussions and press conferences
Observations, on site	Micro situations	Almost all
	Visual patterns	Setting, actors, ecology
	Institutional inventories	Practices, customs, festivals
	Histories	Mostly local
Self-definition	Primacy of local perspective	Themes, values, world view
	Inductive explanations	"Grounded"
	Neologisms	"Positivist" vs "naturalistic"
	Appeal to philosophical texts	Dilthey, Husserl, Shutz, etc.
	Anti-instrumentation	Interviewer the "instrument"
	Ethical issues	Privacy, intimacies
	Specializations	Ethnomethodology, hermeneutics

These attributes are self-explanatory, given a minimal familiarity with the movement. Very likely each item could be divided and refined, but that would run the risk of too many missing cases. "Case studies" are omitted because they overlap with ethnography and, like ethnography, combine several techniques with a product that reflects the analytic and synthetic skills of the single (usually) ethnographer, who is the all-purpose "instrument." Likewise, the table does not show a primary category of "qualitative data analysis" despite the many textbooks with that or a similar title. The techniques in these texts are not distinctive and/or standardized, and would probably defy reliable coding. Techniques of observation are also fuzzy, but they can be distinguished by the object of observation and case-specific use of instruments, such as an air photo or village maps.

Also excluded are computer-based methods of "content" or text analysis, such as those used for the statistical analysis of newspapers and similar "ethnographic" accounts, as well as expressions in novels or focus-group transcripts. More recently, surveillance agencies record and analyze telephone and email communications in their efforts to track terrorists. In an early non-computerized example, comparing folktales, Young (1978) was able to construct measures of folktale content and link these to indicators of U.S. Indian tribal structure. More recent developments are reviewed in Bond (2005) and Roberts (1997).

The quantitative version of content analysis differs in a fundamental way from "narrative analysis" and computerized analysis of field notes used in qualitative analysis. Both approaches distinguish between description and expression, but the qualitative methods for analyzing these two kinds of texts allows the analyst to weave the components together in her mind. As such, the synthesis is inaccessible. By contrast, quantitative content analysis is totally transparent and reliable. As for the use of computers in qualitative analysis, Drisko (2004:189) remarks that "the (high) status of QDA (qualitative data analysis) software is quite striking given that pencil and paper techniques of data analysis can generally be just as effective." What he means is that such programs simply help the researcher to organize the materials, much like a card file. At any rate, there is a clear-cut divide in the two types of computer programs. Miles and Huberman (1994:316) list twenty-two programs dedicated to organizing data, without overlap of those listed in the online articles dealing with quantitative content analysis.

The list in Table 1 includes a category for the many statements of epistemology that qualitative texts contain (e. g., Bryman 1988; Guba 1985; Gubrium and Holstein 1997; Hammersley 2008; Lincoln and Guba

1985). They are relatively infrequent, but they are important in indicating the radical nativist version of qualitative methods, one that draws on obscure past doctrines for justification.

The many examples of neologisms and redefinitions merit a special study of their own. A partial list, based on items in the indexes of several texts, would include: analytic vocabulary, artfulness, bracketing, brute being, close scrutiny, working skepticism, contrast structures, creative interviewing, deprivatization, descriptive authority, descriptive challenges, descriptive richness, thick description, explanatory footings, indexicality, disciplinary intersections, occasioned resources, lived border of reality, making culture local, method talk, narrative horizons, narrative incitement, normal forms, writing strategies, constitutive ethnography, covert observation, deductivism, ecological validity, ethogenics, grounded theory, group interview, in-depth interviewing, activity record, casting nets, composite sequence analysis, contact summary sheet, context chart, data accounting sheet, folk taxonomy. It is true, of course, that all paradigms introduce new terms, but the vocabulary of qualitative methods writers is outstanding in this regard.

The material presented so far supports the classification of qualitative research methods as an intra-disciplinary social movement, but the further classification as "nativistic" requires different arguments. Clearing the ground for these, we note that the qualitative methods movement is not a Kuhnian "paradigm shift" even though, as Hammersley (2008:20ff) summarizes their views, most qualitative sociologists believe that it is. Unlike new theories in physics, biology, and even in sociology, qualitative methods is not a new theory that could replace one already on the books. Rather, it is an across-the-board revision of the discipline. Implementing it would be equivalent to requiring all biology students to do naturalistic studies of the kind Darwin did and making the study of DNA techniques optional.

Another background point is that, aside from some primitive counting in early times, sociology must have begun as questions and answers. Indigenous bands met at the boundaries of their territories and learned about each other via observation and questions in a lingua franca. Contemporary qualitative researchers continue this practice in the many marginal situations that they study. They would also accept the textbook account that the modern history of qualitative methods began with the work of the "Chicago School" studies and that of the British (colonial) ethnographers (Hall 2001). In this generic form, qualitative methods are widely used by social scientists of all persuasions.

But this account misses the recent intensification and "purification" of these generic methods in opposition to the dominant quantitative methodology. Its radical advocates (Lincoln and Guba 1985) imply that qualitative "inquiry" is the only path to understanding the foundations of sociology, which they take to be the complex constructed reality defined by collective beliefs, perceptions, and intentions. But not all these radical advocates of qualitative methods are reaching back to an earlier period for legitimization. Rather, some are digging in their intellectual heels and adamantly resisting the expansion of quantitative methods and, more fundamentally, causal explanation. Thus, they find themselves left behind even if they have not actively turned to the past.

There appear to be three degrees of conservative/nativist thought that apply: There is the traditional conservative, who accepts the dominance of quantification and is satisfied with the optional use of qualitative methods in sociology; the militant conservative, who wants qualitative methods institutionalized by requiring courses in them; and the radical nativist, who aspires to the dominance of qualitative methods, as in anthropology. The third position sees sociology moving in the direction of economics, and claims to have found an alternative philosophical basis for qualitative research. Not surprisingly, they work aggressively to impose it.

An Ecological Theory of Nativism

Focusing on U.S. political currents, Lipset and Raab (1978) identified a basic dynamic in the political groups in the U.S. that applies to nativist groups: "If there has been one constant, it has been the perception of extreme rightist movements as those which have risen primarily in reaction against the displacement of power and status accompanying change; while leftwing extremism has been seen as impelling social change, and in that course, attempting to overthrow old power and status groups" (1978:3). About the same time, Tilly (1975) formulated a typology that applied to peasant groups in European history. He contrasted the reactions of communal versus associationally-organized groups as they acquired, maintained, or lost position in relation to the "structure of power." Those that acquired position responded with for-

ward looking actions, while the losers typically engaged in defensive
activities.

These two formulations are fundamentally ecological in that causality turns on the community's response to the wider social environment.
At any rate, that is the theory template that I have drawn on in formulating a variant explanation. The new version starts with a definition of
organizational strength that turns on the institutionalized capacity for
problem-solving. It has three principal dimensions: the division of labor,
which determines the application of specialized knowledge to the
problem; pluralism in the sense of institutions and groups that facilitate
comparison of divergent policies (a component of democracy); and
mobilization behind a leader or a program that offers a different perspective when the problem is judged to be intractable. These dimensions
can in principle be measured for all levels of community and regardless
of context.

With this definition of organizational capacity, the proposed
explanation may be summarized by the hypothesis that weak communities, from the nation-state on down to academic departments, confronted
by a threat to their existence (or at least the status quo), tend to react with
"nativism," while stronger communities react with "nationalism."
Threats take many forms but shifts in the organization of the community
that marginalizes one or more factions is most relevant here.

Applying the Theory

The existential threat to the discipline is the rapid development of
quantitative methods. Although an analysis of the indicators is beyond
the scope of this article, the expansion of quantitative methods is widely
recognized. Articles in the major journals are now mostly quantitative,
and new fields that have appeared in recent decades, such as historical
studies of strikes and revolutions, are heavily quantitative. Statistical
methods have proliferated and the reference books for statistical pack-
ages have become thicker and more complex.

As was done for qualitative methods, we can list the attributes of an
ideal type. The items were selected from an informal survey of published
articles and amount to another measurement hypothesis. As before, they
are generally familiar.

The theme that runs through this conceptualization of the quantitative program is its tacit claim of invincibility. A consensus on the future

of sociology seems to have crystallized, and quantitative methods (as defined in Table 2) are central to this achievement. Everything else is "social thought," journalism, or simply "stories."

Implicit in this program is the threat of excluding qualitative research from the discipline, following the path taken by economics. Given this combination of weakness and perception of threat on the part of qualitative researchers, they have few choices other than migrating to more tolerant associations or leaving sociology altogether. It is no wonder that they have reached back into the discipline's history for the elements of a counterattack.

Table 2 Primary and secondary attributes of an ideal type definition of quantitative methods

Primary	Secondary	Examples and Comments
Causal analysis	Comparative designs	Cross-sections, longitudinal
	Multivariate statistics	Varied forms of regression
	Tests of hypotheses	Comparisons are essential
	Reliability and validity tests	Measurement is integral
	Qualitative techniques optional	Focus groups, etc. are mainly rhetorical devices
Instrumentation	Sample surveys	Single purpose, general
	Informant surveys	Different from key informants
	Official statistics	UN, World Bank and online
	Experiments	Rare and increasing
Self-definition	Causal explanation	General models preferred
	Realism; relativism rejected	Constructivism allowed
	Intervening processes	Reductionism vs other types
	Replications	Desirable
	Specialization	Increasingly

Conclusion and Discussion

This essay argues that the recent expansion of interest and activity known as "qualitative methods" is a nativist social movement and can be explained as the response of communities to an existential threat. As such, it is a non-violent example of a type of movement that appears in all eras and at all levels of community.

Most sociologists will accept the classification of qualitative methods as a (small) social movement, because such mobilizations are familiar in all intellectual disciplines where they are called "schools," or "paradigms." Their accepted purpose is to enhance the discipline and to generate new job opportunities, grants, and promotions. The brief enthusiasm for "social indicators research" in the 1980s is an example on the quantitative side, and there are others, such as organizational ecology and new institutional economic sociology. But the qualitative methods movement is different from these in its nativistic drive to institutionalize the many informally accepted qualitative techniques in sociology. In short, it aspires to change the definition of the discipline by influencing any and all specialties within it.

Will its momentum begin to slow when some kind of accommodation is reached? And what kind of accommodation can have that effect? If the interaction hypothesis is correct, a reduction of the threat and/or strengthening the weaker faction in sociology should reduce nativism. As it happens, there is a trend in some sociology departments that will bring about both these changes. To judge by the many and multiple editions of textbooks in qualitative methods, courses in this subject are proliferating at both the undergraduate and graduate levels. These classes must be staffed and the faculty integrated into the departmental structure. In some of these departments, we may be sure, doctorates are awarded on the basis of qualitative research and tenure given to the those who become faculty. Such a development ought to result in a new equilibrium and a reduction of nativism. Is this too high a price for departments to pay? Some will think so, and the dominant quantitative researchers will mobilize the disciplinary "immune system" against this "disease." But other departments, especially those in applied fields, will accept it, and all members will learn to live with each other, very much as religious differences are smoothed over in many countries.

REFERENCES

Note: the references under "Young" contain the detailed information that the respective journal copyright owners require of authors.

Aberle, David F. 1963. "The Incest Taboo and Mating Patterns of Animals." *American Anthropologist* LXV:253-265.

Adler, Nancy E., and Joan M. Ostrove. 1999. "SES and Health: What We Know and What We Don't Know," in *Socioeconomic Status and Health in Industrial Nations: Psychological and Biological Pathways* (pp. 13-15), edited by N. E. Adler, M. Marmot, G. S. McEwen, and J. Stewart. New York: New York Academy of Sciences.

Aiken, Michael, and Paul E. Mott. 1970. "Introduction: Factors Influencing Configurations of Power," in *The Structure of Community Power*, edited by M. Aiken. New York: Random House.

Aiken, Michael, and Robert R. Alford. 1970. "Community Structure and Innovation: The Case of Urban Renewal. *American Sociological Review 35*: 650-665.

Allen, John C., and Don A. Dillman. 1994. *Against All Odds: Rural Community in the Information Age*. Jackson, TN: Westview Press.

Almond, Gabriel A., and Sidney Verba. 1963. *The Civic Culture: Political Attitudes and Democracy in Five Nations*. Princeton, NJ: Princeton University Press.

Alvarez-Dardet C., Ruiz, MT., Thomas McKeown and Archibald Cochrane: 1993. "A Journey Through the Diffusion of Their Ideas." *BMJ 306*: 1252-5.

Anderson, Eugene N., Felix Medina Tzuc, and Pastor Valdez Chale. 2005. *Political Ecology in a Yucatec Maya Community*. Tucson, AZ: University of Arizona Press.

Anderson, Norman B., and Cherl A. Armstead. 1995. "Toward Understanding the Association of Socioeconomic Status and Health: A New challenge for the Bio Psychological Approach." *Psychosomatic Medicine* 57:213-225.

Anuario Estadístico Instituto Nacional de Estadística, Geografía e Informática. 2005. http://www.inegi.org.mx/
_____. 2004. *La Población Hablante de Lengua Indígena de Yucatán*.

_____. 1982. *Localidades Pobladas. XI Censo Nacional de Pob-lación y de Vivienda.* http://www.inegi.org.mx/

_____. 1986-1988. *Demografía.* http://www.inegi.org.mx/

Bartels, Larry M. 2006. "What's the Matter with What's the Matter with Kansas?" *Quarterly Journal of Political Science. Quarterly Journal of Political Science* 1: 2001-226.

Becquart-Leclercq, Jeanne. 1988. *La Démocratie Locale à l'Améri-caine.* Paris: GRAL.

Bell, Daniel, (ed.) 2002. *The Radical Right.* New Brunswick, NJ: Transaction Publishers.

Bennis, Warren, and Hallum Movius. 2006. "Why Harvard Is so Hard to Lead." *Chronicle of Higher Education* 52:B20.

Berkman, Lisa F., and Kawachi Berkman (eds.). 2000. *Social Epidemi-ology.* New York: Oxford University Press.

Berkman, Lisa F., Thomas Glass, Ian Brissette, and Teresa Seeman. 2000. "From Social Integration to Health: Durkheim in the New Millennium." *Social Science and Medicine* 51 (6):843-57.

Bogue, Donald J. 1961. "The Structure of the Metropolitan Com-munity," in *Studies in Human Ecology*, edited by G. A. Theodorson. Chicago: Row, Peterson.

Bollen, Kenneth A. 1980. "Issues in the Comparative Measurement of Political Democracy." *American Sociological Review* 45:370-390.

Bond, Doug. 2005. "Content Analysis," in *Encyclopedia of Social Measurement,* edited by K. Dempf Leonard. New York: Elsevier.

Bricker, Victoria, R. 1981. *The Indian Christ, the Indian King.* Austin: University of Texas Press.

Brunner, E. 1997. "Stress and the Biology of Inequality." *British Medi-cal Journal* 314:1472-1476.

Bryman, Alan. 1988. *Quantity and Quality in Social Research.* New York: Routledge.

Buchanan, Patrick J. 2012. *Suicide of a Superpower.* New York: Thomas Dunne Books.

Bunge, Mario. 2009. *Causality and Modern Science.* New Brunswick, N.J.: Transaction Publishers.

Bunker, John P., Deanna S. Gomby, and Barbara H. Kehrer. 1989. *Pathways to Health.* Menlo Park, CA: The Henry J. Kaiser Family Foundation.

Burns, Allen F. 1977. "The Caste War in the 1970's: Present Day Accounts from a Village in Quintana Roo," in *Anthropology and History in Yucatan*, edited by Grant D. Jones. Austin: University of Texas Press.

Caldwell, John C. 1986. "Routes to Low Mortality in Poor Countries." *Population and Development Review* 12:171-220.

_____. 1989. "Mass Education as a Determinant of Mortality Decline," in *Selected Readings in the Cultural, Social and Behavioral Determinants of Health: Health Series No. 1*, edited by J. C. Caldwell, and G. Santow. Canberra: Australian National University.

Cameron, Euan. 2006. "Introduction," in *The Sixteenth Century*, edited by Euan Cameron. New York: Oxford University Press.

Canovan, Margaret. 1985. "Populism," in *The Social Science Encyclopedia* (pp. 628-29), edited by Adam Kuper and Jessica Kuper. New York: Routledge and Kegan Paul.

Cardoso, Fernando H., and Enzo Faletto. 1979. *Dependency and Development in Latin America*. Berkeley: University of California Press.

Carroll, M. P. 1975. "Revitalization Movements and Social Structure: Some Quantitative Tests." *American Sociological Review* 40:389-401.

Centers for Disease Control and Prevention (CDC). *Query year: 2012*. CDC WONDER Online Database. Compressed Mortality File. http: www.cdc.gov.

Chapple, Elliot, and Carleton Coon. 1953. *Principles of Anthropology*. New York: Henry Holt and Company.

Chen, M. K., and F. Lowenstein. 1985. "The Physician-Population Ratio as a Proxy Measure of the Adequacy of Health Care." *International Journal of Epidemiology* 14: 300-3.

Clarke, Leslie L., Frank L. Farmer, and Michael K. Miller. 1994. "Structural Determinants of Infant Mortality in Metropolitan and Nonmetropolitan America." *Rural Sociology* 59:84-99.

Clemente, Frank, and Richard U. Sturgis. 1972. "The Division of Labor in America and Ecological Analysis." *Social Forces* 51:176-181.

Cochrane, Archibald, A. S. St Leger, and Frank Moore. 1978. "Health Service 'Input' and Mortality 'Output' in Developed Countries." *Journal of Epidemiology of Community Health* 32:200-205.

Cooper, R., M. Steinhauer, A. Schatzkin, and W. Miller. 1981. "Improved Mortality smong U.S. Blacks, 1968-1978: The Role of Antiracist Struggle." *International Journal of Health Services* 11: 511-522.

Coult, Allan D. 1963. "Causality and Cross-sex Prohibitions." *American Anthropologist* LXV:266-277.

Cutler, D. M., and A. Lleras-Muney. 2008. "Education and Health: Evaluating Theories and Evidence, in *Making Americans Healthier* (pp. 29-60), edited by Robert Schoeni, James House, George Kaplan, and Harold Pollack. New York: Russell Sage Foundation.

Dahl, Robert A. 1971. *Polyarchy Participation and Opposition.* New Haven, CT: Yale University Press.

Diamond, Jared. 1997. *Guns, Germs and Steel: The Fates of Human Societies.* New York: W.W. Norton.

Denzin, Norman K., and Ynonna S. Lincoln (eds.) 1994. *Handbook of Qualitative Research.* Thousand Oaks, CA: Sage.

Dickerson, S. S., and M. E. Kemeny. 2004. "Acute Stressors and Cortisol Responses: A Theoretical Integration and Synthesis of Laboratory Research." *Psychological Bulletin* 130(3): 355-391.

Diez-Roux, Ana V. 1998. "Bringing Context Back into Epidemiology: Variables and Fallacies in Multilevel Analysis." *American Journal of Public Health* 88:216-222.

Drisko, James W. 2004. "Qualitative Data Analysis Software," in *The Qualitative Research Experience,* edited by K. K. Padgett. Boston: Thomson Learning.

Dubos, Renee. 1959. *Mirage of Health.* New York: Harper & Brothers.

Dumond, D. E. 1970. "Competition, Cooperation, and the Folk Society." *Southwestern Journal of Anthropology* 26:261-286.

Dundes, Alan. 1964. *The Morphology of North American Folktales.* Helsinki: Folklore Fellows Communications.

Durkheim, Emile. 1951 [1897]. *Suicide: A Study in Sociology.* Glencoe, IL: The Free Press.

_____. 1954 [1912]. *The Elementary Forms of the Religious Life.* Glencoe, IL: The Free Press.

Dutton, Diana B, and Sol Levine. 1989. "Socioeconomic Status and Health: Overview, Methodological Critique and Reformation," in *Pathways to Health*, edited By J. P. Bunker, D.S. Gomby, and B. H. Kehrer. Menlo Park, CA: The Henry J. Kaiser Family Foundation.

Elo, Irma T., and Samuel H. Preston. 1996. "Educational Differentials in Mortality: United States 1979-1985." *Social Science and Medicine* 42:47-57.

Evans, Robert G., Morris L. Barer, and Theodore R. Marmor. 1994. *Why Are Some People Healthy and Others Not?* Hawthorne, NY: Aldine De Gruyter.

Farhang, M. 1988. "Fundamentalism and Civil Rights in Contemporary Middle Eastern Politics," in *Human Rights and the World's Religions*, edited by L. S. Rouner. Notre Dame, IA: University of Notre Dame Press.

Feldman, Jacob J., Deiane M. Makuc, Joel C. Kleinman, and Joan Cornoni-Huntley. 1989. "National Trends in Educational Differentials in Mortality." *American Journal of Epidemiology* 129:919-933.

Feldman, Noah. 2008. *The Fall and Rise of the Islamic State*. Princeton, NJ: Princeton University Press.

Fogel, Robert. 2000. *Fourth Great Awakening and the Future of Egalitarianism.* Chicago: University of Chicago Press.

Fowler, Irving. 1964. *Local Industrial Structures, Economic Power and Community Welfare*. Totowa, NJ: Bedminster Press.

Frank, A. G. 1970. "The Development of Underdevelopment," in *Imperialism and Underdevelopment* (pp. 4-17), edited by Robert I. Rhodes. New York: Monthly Review Press.

Frank, Thomas. 2004. *What's the Matter with Kansas? How Conservatives Won the Heart of America.* New York: Henry Holt and Co.

Freeman, Derek. 1983. *Samoa: The Making and Unmaking of an Anthropological Myth*. Cambridge, MA: Harvard University Press.

Galea, S. (ed.). 2007. *Macrosocial Determinants of Population Heath.* New York: Springer.

Gallaher, Arthur Jr. 1980. "Dependence on External Authority and the Decline of Community," in *The Dying Community* (pp. 85-108), edited by Arthur Gallaher Jr., and Harland Padfield. Albuquerque: University of New Mexico Press.

Gaquin, Deirdre A., and Mary Meghan Ryan (eds). 2004. *County and City Data Book Extra: 2002, 2004*. Lanham, MD: Berman Press.

Gilles, Jere Lee, and Michael Dalecki. 1988. "Rural Well-Being and Agricultural Change in Two Farming Regions." Rural Sociology 53:40-55.

Goldschmidt, Walter. 1978a [1946]. *As You Sow: Three Studies in the Social Consequences of Agri-Business*. Montclair, NJ: Allanheld, Osmun & Co.

_____. 1978b. "Large-Scale Farming and the Rural Social Structure." *Rural Sociology* 43:362-66.

Goodchilds, Jacqueline D., and John Harding. 1960. "Formal Organizations and informal Activities." *Journal of Social Issues* XVI:16-28.

Grantham, Dewey W. 1994. *The South in Modern America*. New York: Harpercollins.

Great Geographical Atlas. 1982. Chicago, IL: Rand Mcnally & Co., in Association with Instituto Geográfico De Agostini and Mechell Beazley Publishers.

Guba, Egon G. 1985. "The Context of Emergent Paradigm Research," in *Organizational Theory and Inquiry*, edited by Y. Lincoln. Thousand Oaks, CA: Sage Publications.

Gubrium, Jaber F., and James A. Holstein. 1997. *The New Language of Qualitative Method*. New York: Oxford University Press.

Haan, Mary N., George A. Kaplan, and S. Leonard Syme. 1989. "Socioeconomic Status and Health: Old Observations and New Thoughts," in *Pathways to Health*, edited by J. P. Bunker, D. S. Gomby, and B. H. Kehrer. Menlo Park, CA: The Henry J. Kaiser Family Foundation.

Halebsky, Sandor. 1976. *Mass Society and Political Conflict: Toward a Reconstruction of Theory*. New York: Cambridge University Press.

Hall, J. R. 2001. "Qualitative Methods, History of," in *International Encyclopedia of the Social & Behavioral Sciences*, edited by Neil Smelser, and P. B. Baltes. New York: Elsevier.

Hammersley, Martyn. 2008. *Questioning Qualitative Inquiry: Critical Essays*. Thousand Oaks, CA: Sage Publications.

Harris, Craig K., and J. Gilbert. 1982. "Large-Scale Farming, Rural Income, and Goldschmidt's Agrarian Thesis." *Rural Sociology* 47:449-58.

Hawley, Amos H. 1950. *Human Ecology: A Theory of Community Structure*. New York: Ronald.

Hawley, Amos H. 1984. "Human Ecological and Marxian Theories." *American Journal of Sociology* 89:904-917.

Hertzman, Clyde, Shona Kelly, and Martin Bobak. 1996. *East-West Life Expectancy Gap in Europe*. Alphen aan den Rijn, the Netherlands: Kluwer Academic Publishers.

Hibbs, Douglas A. Jr. 1973. *Mass Political Violence: A Cross-National Causal Analysis*. New York: John Wiley & Sons.

Hirschman, Albert O. 1970. *Exit Voice and Loyalty: Responses to Decline in Firms, Organizations and States*. Cambridge, MA: Harvard University Press.

Hobbs, Daryl. 1995. "Social Organization in the Countryside," in *The Changing American Countryside* (pp. 369-96), edited by Emery N. Castle. Lawrence: University of Kansas Press.

Hofstadter, Richard. 1965. "The Paranoid Style in American Politics," in his *The Paranoid Style in American Politics and Other Essays*. New York: Alfred A. Knopf.

Hostettler, Ueli. 1995. "Changing Socioeconomic Stratification: The Day of Central Quintana Roo," in *The Fragmented Present Mesoamerican Societies Facing Modernization* (pp. 137-149), edited by Ruth Gubler, and Ueli Hosteller. Germany: Verlag Anton Saurwein, Markt Schwaben.

Instituto National De Estadisticas. 1975-1976, V Censo Nacional Agropecuario. Santiago, http://www.inegi.org.mx/

____. 1982. Localidades Pobladas. X! Censo Nadonal De Poblacion Y De Vivienda. http://www.inegi.org.mx/

____. 1986-1988. Demografia. http://www.inegi.org.mx/

____. "1989-1990. Estadisticas Agropecuarias." http://www.inegi.org.mx/

Jayachandran, J. and G. K. Jarvis. 1986. "Socioeconomic Development, Medical Care and Nutrition as Determinants of Infant Mortality in Less Developed Countries." *Journal of Social Biology* 33:301-15.

Johansen, Harley E., and Glenn V. Fuguitt. 1984. *The Changing Rural Village in America: Demographic and Economic Trends since 1950*. Pensacola, FL: Ballinger Publishing Company.

Jones, G. D. 1974 "Revolution and Continuity in Santa Cruz Maya Society." *American Ethnologist* 1:659-683.

Juergensmeyer, Mark. 2008. *Global Rebellion*. Berkeley: University of California Press.

Kaplan, G. A., N. Ranjit, and S. A. Burgard. 2008. "Lifting Gates, Lengthening Lives: Did Civil Rights Policies Improve The Health of African American Women in the 1960s and 1970s?" in *Making Americans Healthier* (pp. 145-169), edited by R. F. Schoeni J. S. House, G. A. Kaplan, and H. Pollack. New York: Russell Sage.

Kaplan, George A. 2001. "Economic Policy Is Health Policy: Findings from the Study of Income, Socioeconomic Status, and Health," in *Income, Socioeconomic Status, and Health*, edited by A. A. Auerback, and B. K. Krimgold. Washington, DC: National Policy Association, Academy for Health Research and Health Policy.

Kaplan, George A., Elsie R. Pamuk, John W. Lynch, Richard D. Cohen and Jennifer I. Balfour. 1996. "Inequality in Income and Mortality in the United States: Analysis of Mortality and Potential Pathways." *British Medical Journal* 312:999-1003.

Kaplan, Robert M. 2000. "Promoting Wellness: Biomedical Versus Outcomes Models," in *Promoting Wellness: New Frontiers for Research, Practice, and Policy*, edited by M. S. Jammer, and D. Stokois. Berkeley: University of California Press.

Kaufmann, Eric P. 2004. *The Rise and Fall of Anglo-America.* Cambridge, MA: Harvard University Press.

Kawachi, Ichiro, Bruce P. Kennedy, and Richard G. Wilkinson (eds.) 1999. *The Society and Population Health Reader: Income Inequality and Health.* New York: New Press.

Kazin, Michael. 1995. *The Populist Persuasion.* NY: Basic Books.

Kehoe, A. B. 2006. *The Ghost Dance.* Long Grove, IL: Waveland Press.

Kepel, Giles. 1994. *The Revenge of God: The Resurgence of Islam, Christianity and Judaism in the Modern World.* University Park: Pennsylvania State University Press.

——. 2004. *The War for Muslim Minds.* Cambridge, MA: Harvard University Press.

Key, V. O. Jr. 1951. *Southern Politics in State and Nation.* New York: Knopf.

Kitagawa, Evelyn M., and Philip M. Hauser. 1973. *Differential Mortality in the United States: A Study in Socioeconomic Epidemiology.* Cambridge, MA: Harvard University Press.

Kornhauser, William. 1959. *The Politics of Mass Society.* Glencoe, IL: The Free Press.

Kuhn, Thomas A. 1970. *The Structure of Scientific Revolutions*. Chicago: University of Chicago Press

Lamis, Alexander P. 1999. *Southern Politics in the 1990s*. Baton Rouge: Louisiana State University Press.

Lanz, Paula, James S. House, James Lepkowski, David R. Williams, Richard P. Mero, and Jieming Chen. 1998. "Socioeconomic Factors, Health Behaviors, and Mortality." *Journal of the American Medical Association* 279:1703-1708.

Lenski, Gerhard. 2005. *Ecological-Evolutionary Theory*. Boulder, CO: Paradigm Publishers.

Levin, Lisa. 1996. *Human Rights: Questions and Answers*. New York: UNESCO Publishing.

Levi-Strauss, Claude. 1967. "The Story of Asdiwal," in *The Structural Study of Myth and Totemism*, edited by I E. Leach. London: Tavistock Publications.

Levi-Strauss, Claude. 1967. *Structural Anthropology*. New York: Doubleday and Co.

———. 1968. *L'Origine des Manières de Table*. Paris, France: Plon.

Lewis, Oscar. 1951. *Life in a Mexican Village: Tepotzlan Restudied*. Champaign: University of Illinois Press.

Lincoln, Yvonna S., and Egon G. Guba. 1985. *Naturalistic Inquiry*. Thousand Oaks, CA: Sage Publications.

Link, Bruce G. and Phelan, Jo. 1995. "Social Conditions as Fundamental Causes of Disease." *Journal of Health and Social Behavior* Extra Issue: 80-94.

Linton R. 1958 /1943. "Nativistic Movements," in *Reader in Comparative Religion* (pp. 466-475), edited by W. Lessa, and E. Z. Vogt. Evanston, IL: Row, Peterson and Co.

Lipset S. M., and R. Raab. 1978/1970. *The Politics of Unreason, Right-Wing Extremism in America*. Chicago: University of Chicago Press.

Little, David, John Kelsay, and Abdulaziz A. Sachedina. 1998. *Human Rights and the Conflict of Cultures: Western and Islamic Perspectives on Religious Liberty*. Columbia: University of South Carolina Press.

Lobao, Linda M. 1990. *Locality and Inequality: Farm and Industry Structure and Socioeconomic Conditions*. Albany: State University of New York Press.

Lomas, Johathan. 1998. "Social Capital and Health: Implications for Public Health and Epidemiology." *Social Science and Medicine* 47:1181-1188.

Lynch, John W., George Kaplan, and Richard Cohen. 1994. "Childhood and Adult Socioeconomic Status as Predictors of Mortality in Finland." *The Lancet* 343:524-527.

Lynch, John W., Richard A. Cohen, Jakka Tuomilehto, Jukka Salonen, and George Kaplan. 1996. "Do Cardiovascular Risk Factors Explain the Relation between Socioeconomic Status, Rates of All-Cause Mortality, Cardiovascular Mortality, and Acute Myocardial Infarction?" *American Journal of Epidemiology* 144:934-942.

Lynd, Robert S., and Helen M. Lynd. 1929. *Middletown: A Study in Contemporary American Culture*. New York: Harcourt Brace.

MacEoin, Denis. 2009. *Sharia Law or One Law for All*. London: Civitas: Institute for the Study of Civil Society.

Macintyre, Sally. 1997. "The Black Report and Beyond: What Are the Issues?" *Social Science and Medicine* 44:723-45.

Mackenbach, J. P., M. H. Bouvier-Colle, and E. Jougla. 1990. "Avoidable Mortality and Health Services: A Review of Aggregate Data Studies." *Journal of Epidemiology Community Health* 44:106-111.

Mackenbach, Johan, M. J. Bakker, Anton E. Kunst, and F. Diderichsen. 2002. "Socioeconomic Inequalities in Health in Europe: An Overview," in *Reducing Inequalities in Health: A European Perspective* (pp. 3-24), edited by J. Mackenback, and M. Bakker. New York: Routledge.

Maharidge, Dale. 1996. *The Coming White Minority: California's Eruptions and America's Future*. New York: Times Books.

Malinowski, Bronislaw. 1931. "Culture". *Encyclopedia of the Social Sciences*. New York: Macmillan.

Marmot, M. G., Martin Bobak, and George Davey Smith. 1995. "Explanations for Social Inequalities in Health," in *Society and Health* (pp. 172-210), edited by B. C. Amick, S. Levine, A. R. Tarlov, and D.C. Walsh. New York: Oxford University Press.

Marmot, Michael, Carol D. Ryff, Larry L. Burnpass, Martin Shipley, and Nadinef. Marks. 1997. "Social Inequalities in Health: Next Questions and Converging Evidence." *Social Science and Medicine* 44:901-910.

Marshall, John Urquhart. 1969. *The Location of Service Towns.* Toronto: University of Toronto Press.

Matthews, Robert. 2000. "Storks Deliver Babies (P=.008)." *Teaching Statistics* 33: 36-38.

Mayer, A. E. 1999. *Islam and Human Rights.* Jackson, TN: Westview Press.

McEwen, Bruce S., and Teresa Seeman. 1999. "Protective and Damaging Effects of Mediators of Stress," in *Socioeconomic Status and Health in Industrial Nations: Social, Psychological and Biological Pathways,* edited by N. Adler, M. Marmot, B.S. Mcewen, and J. Steward. New York: The New York Academy of Sciences.

McGinnis, Michael, and William Foege. 1993. "Actual Causes of Death in the United States." *Journal of American Medical Association* 270:2207-2212.

Mckeown, Thomas. 1976. *The Role of Medicine: Dream, Mirage or Nemesis.* London: Nuffield Provincial Hospital Trust.

Mckinlay, John, and Sonja Mckinlay. 1977. "The Questionable Contribution of Medical Measures to Decline of Mortality in the United States in the Twentieth Century." *Milbank Memorial Fund Quarterly* 55:405-428.

Menzel, Herbert. 1950. "Comment on Robinson's Ecological Correlations and the Behavior of Individuals." *American Sociological Review* 15:674.

Middleton, Russell. 1962. "Brother-Sister and Father-Daughter Marriage in Ancient Egypt." *American Sociological Review* XXVII:603-611.

Mielck, A., H. Graham, and S. Bremberg. 2002. "Children, an Important Target Group for the Reduction of Socioeconomic Inequalities," in *Reducing Inequalities in Health: A European Perspective* (pp. 144-168), edited by J. Mackenbach, and M. Bakker. New York: Routledge.

Miles, Matthew B., and A. Michael Huberman. 1994. *Qualitative Data Analysis.* Thousand Oaks, CA: Sage Publications.

Mills, C. Wright, and Melville J. Ulmer. 1970. "Small Business and Civic Welfare," in *The Structure of Community Power* (pp. 124-154), edited by Michael Aiken, and P. E. Mott. New York: Random House.

Mokdad, A. H., J. S. Marks, D. F. Stroup, and Julie L. Gerberding. 2004. "Actual Causes of Death in the United States, 2000." *Journal of the American Medical Association* 291:1238-1245.

Mooney, James. 1991/1896. *The Ghost-Dance Religion and the Sioux Outbreak of 1890.* Lincoln: University of Nebraska Press.

Morgan, Michael C. 2010. "The Seventies and the Rebirth of Human Rights," in *The Shock of The Global,* edited by C. S. Maier, Erez Manela, and D. J. Sargent. Cambridge, MA: Harvard University Press.

Mosley, Henry W., and Lincoln C. Chen. 1984. "An Analytical Framework for the Study of Child Survival in Developing Countries." *Population and Development Review* 10:25-45.

Mullett, M. 1984. *The Counter-Reformation and the Catholic Reformation in Early Modern Europe.* New York: Methuen.

Murdock, George P. 1949. *Social Structure.* New York: Macmillan.

Murray, Jocelyn (ed.). 1982. *Cultural Atlas of Africa.* New York: Facts On File, Inc.

Nahirny, Vladimir C. 1962. "Some Observations on Ideological Groups." *American Journal of Sociology* LXVIII: 398-402.

Nimer, M. 2007. "Islamophobia and Anti-Americanism Are Mutually Reinforcing," in his *Islamophobia and Anti-Americanism.* Beltsville, MD: Amana Publications.

Nisbet, Robert A. 1953. *The Quest for Community.* New York: Oxford University Press.

Nojumi, N. 2008. "The Rise and Fall of the Taliban," in *The Taliban and the Crisis of Afghanistan* (pp. 90-117), edited by Robert D. Crews and Amin Tarzi. Cambridge, MA: Harvard University Press.

Oakes, J. M., and P. H. Rossi. 2003. "The Measurement of SES in Health Research: Current Practice and Steps toward a New Approach." *Social Science and Medicine* 56:769-784.

O'Conner, Anthony. 1983. *The African City.* New York: Africana Publishing Co.

Pappas, Gregory, Susan Queen, Wilbur Hadden, and Gail Fisher. 1993. "The Increasing Disparity in Mortality between Socioeconomic Groups in the US, 1950 and 1986." *New England Journal of Medicine* 329:103-109.

Park, Robert E. 1952/1936. "Human Ecology," in *Human Communities, the City and Human Ecology* (pp. 145-158), edited by Everett C. Hughes. Glencoe: IL: The Free Press.

Pearlin, Leonard I., and Carmi Schooler. 1978. "The Structure of Coping." *Journal of Health and Social Behavior* 19:2-21.

Phelan, Jo C., Bruce G. Link, and P. Tehranifar. 2010. "Social Conditions as Fundamental Causes of Health inequalities: Theory, Evidence and Policy Implications." *Journal of Health and Social Behavior* 51:S28-S40.

Postel, Charles. 2007. *The Populist Vision*. New York: Oxford University Press.

Prothrow-Stith, D. and M. Weissman. 1999. *Deadly Consequences*. New York: HarperCollins.

Putnam, Robert D. 1993. *Making Democracy Work*. Princeton, NJ: Princeton University Press.

_____. 2000. *Bowling Alone: The Collapse and Revival of American Community*. New York: Simon and Schuster.

Rasmussen, Scott, and Douglas Schoen. 2010. *Mad as Hell*. New York: HarperCollins.

Redfield, Robert. 1941. *The Folk Culture of Yucatan.* Chicago: University of Chicago Press.

——. 1950. *A Village that Chose Progress: Chan Kom Revisited.* Chicago: The University of Chicago Press.

Reed, N. 2001. *The Caste War of Yucatan,* Stanford, CA: Stanford University Press.

Reichard, Gladys. 1921. "Literary Types and the Dissemination of Myths." *Journal of American Folklore* 34:269-307.

Rich, George. 1971. "Rethinking the Star Husbands." *Journal of American Folklore* 84:436-441.

Richards, Robert O. 1978. "Urbanization of Rural Areas," in *Handbook of Contemporary Urban Life*, edited by David Street. San Francisco: Jossey-Bass.

Robert, S. A., and J. S. House. 2000. "Socioeconomic Inequalities in Health: Integrating Individual, Community, and Societal-Level Theory and Research," *Handbook of Social Studies in Health and Medicine* (pp. 115-35), edited by G. L. Albrecht, R. Fitzpatrick, and S. C. Scrimshaw. Thousand Oaks, CA. Sage Publications.

Roberts, Carl W. 1997. *Text Analysis for the Social Sciences*. Mahwah, NJ: Lawrence Erlbaum Associates.

Rosenberg, Alex, and Daniel W. McShea. 2008. *Philosophy of Biology*. New York: Routledge.

Ross, Catherine E., and Chia-Ling Wu. 1995. "The Links between Education and Health." *American Sociological Review* 60:719-745.

Ruiz, Alvarez-Dardet C. 1993. "Thomas McKeown and Archibald Cochrane: A Journey through the Diffusion of Their Ideas." *British Medical Journal* 306:1252-5

Sampson, Robert J., and William J. Wilson. 1995. "Toward A Theory of Race, Crime, and Urban inequality," in *Crime and Inequality* (pp. 37-54), edited by J. Hagan, and R. D. Peterson. Stanford, CA: Stanford University Press.

Scheuer, M. 2004. *Imperial Hubris*. Washington, D.C.: Brassey's, Inc.

Schilling, Heinz. 2008. *Early Modern European Civilization and Its Political and Cultural Dynamism*. Hanover, NH: University Press of New England.

Schmitt, Eric and Thom Shanker. 2011. *Counterstrike*. New York: Times Books.

Schnore, Leo F. 1958. "Social Morphology and Human Ecology." *American Journal of Sociology* LXIII:620-634.

Schoeni, R., J. House, G. Kaplan, and H. Pollack. 2008. *Making Americans Healthier: Social and Economic Policy as Health Policy*. New York: Russell Sage Foundation.

Schrag, Peter. 2010. *Not Fit for Our Society: Nativism and Immigration*. Berkeley: University of California Press.

Scott, Tom. 2006. "The Economy in Euan Cameron," in *The Sixteenth Century*, edited by Tom Scott. New York: Oxford University Press.

Searle, Clive. 2001. *Qualitative Research*. Chicago, IL: Fitzroy Dearborn Publishers.

Searle, G. W. 1974. *The Counter Reformation*. London: University of London Press.

Seeman, Teresa E., and Bruce S. McEwen. 1996. "Impact of Social Environment Characteristics on Neuroendocrine Regulation." *Psychosomatic Medicine* 58:459-471.

Selye, Hans. 1956. *The Stress of Life*. New York: McGraw-Hill.

Selznick, Philip. 1996. "In Search of Community," in *Rooted in the Land* (pp. 195-203), edited by W. Vitek, and W. Jackson. New Haven: Yale University Press.

Shils, Edward A. 1962. "The Theory of Mass Society." *Diogenes* 39:45-66.

Skees, Jerry R., and L. E. Swanson. 1989. *Farm Structure and Rural Well-Being in the South: Agriculture and Community Change in the U.S.* Jackson, TN: Westview Press.

Skocpol, Theda, and Vanessa Williamson. 2012. *The Tea Party and the Remaking of Republican Conservatism.* New York: Oxford University Press.

Small Farm Viability Project. 1977. *The Family Farm in California: Report of the Small Farm Viability Project.* Sacramento, CA: Governor's Office of Planning and Research.

Southwood, Kenneth E. 1978. "Substantive Theory and Statistical Interaction: Five Models." *American Journal of Sociology* 83:1154-1203.

State of New York. 1981. *State Mandates to Counties.* Albany, NY: Legislative Commission on Expenditure Review.

Summers, Gene F. 1986. "Rural Community Development." *Annual Review of Sociology* 12:347-371.

Swain, Carol M. 2002. *The New White Nationalism in America: Its Challenge To Integration.* New York: Cambridge University Press.

Swanson, Guy E. 1976. "Orpheus and Star Husband: Meaning and the Structure of Myths." *Ethnology* 15:115-133.

Swanson, Louis E. 1989. "Farm and Community Change: A Brief Introduction to the Regional Studies," in *Agriculture and Community Change in the U.S.* (pp. 1-14), edited by L. Swanson. Jackson, TN: Westview Press.

Syme, S. Leonard. 1996. "To Prevent Disease: The Need for a New Approach," in *Health and Social Organization towards a Health Policy for the Twenty-First Century* (pp. 21-31), edited by D. Blane, E. Brunner, and R. Wilkinson. New York: Routledge.

Syme, S. Leonard, and Lisa F. Berkman. 1976. "Social Class, Susceptibility and Sickness." *American Journal of Epidemiology* 104:1-9.

Talmon, Yonina. 1964. "Mate Selection in Collective Settlements." *American Sociological Review* 29:491-508.

Thoits, Peggy A. 1994. "Stressors and Problem-Solving: The Individual as Psychological Activist." *Journal of Health and Social Behavior* 5:143-159.

————. 2010. "Stress and Health: Major Findings and Policy Implica-
    tions." *Journal of Health and Social Behavior* 51
    (Supplement):S41-53.
Thompson, Stith. 1953. "The Star Husband Tale," in *The Study of Folk-
    lore* (pp. 414-474), edited by Allan Dundes. Englewood Cliffs, NJ:
    Prentice Hall.
Tibi, B. 2002. *The Challenge of Fundamentalism*. Berkeley: University
    of California Press.
Tilly, Charles. 1975 [1969]. "Collective Violence in European Perspec-
    tive," in *Violence in America*, edited by H. D. Graham, and Ted R.
    Gurr. New York: Bantam.
Tocqueville, Alexis De. 1954. *Democracy in America*. New York: Vin-
    tage Books.
Tomaskovic-Devey, Donald, and Vincent J. Roscigno. 1997. "Uneven
    Development and Local Inequality in the U.S. South: The Role of
    Outside investment, Landed Elites, and Racial Dynamics." *Socio-
    logical Forum* 12:565-597.
Toth, James. 2005. "Local Islam Gone Global: The Roots of Religious
    Militancy in Egypt and Its Transnational Transformation," in
    Social Movements: An Anthropological Reader, edited by June
    Nash. Hoboken, NJ: Blackwell Publishing.
Turner, R. J., D. A. Lloyd, and B. Wheaton. 1995. "The Epidemiology
    of Social Stress." *American Sociological Review*, 60:104-125.
United Nations Development Programme. 2005. *Arab Human
    Development Report*. New York: United Nations Publications.
Van Dyke, Nella, and Sarah A. Soule. 2002. "Structural Social Change
    and the Mobilizing Eeffect of Threat: Explaining Levels of Patriot
    and Militia Organization in the United States." *Social Problems*
    49:497-520.
Vidich, Arthur J. 1980. "Revolutions in Community Structure," in *The
    Dying Community* (p. 109), edited by Art Gallaher, Jr., and
    Harland Padfield. Albuquerque, NM: University of New Mexico
    Press.
Vidich, Arthur J., and Joseph Bensman. 1958. *Small Town in Mass
    Society*. Princeton, NJ: Princeton University Press.
Villa Rojas, A. 1977. "El Proceso de Integración Nacional entre los
    Mayas de Quintana Roo." *América Indígena* XXXVII:883-905.
Wallace, A. F. C. 1956. "Revitalization Movements." *American
    Anthropologist* 58:264-281.

Walters, Ronald W. 2003. *White Nationalism, Black Interests*. Detroit. MI: Wayne State University Press.

Warren, Roland L. 1978. *The Community in America*. New York: Rand McNally.

Weber, Max. 1946. *From Max Weber: Essays in Sociology*. New York: Oxford University Press.

Wheaton, Blair. 1985. "Models for the Stress-Buffering Functions of Coping Resources." *Journal of Health and Social Behavior* 26:352-364.

Whitaker, B. 2009. *What's Really Wrong with the Middle East*. London: SAQI.

Wilcox, Clifford. 2004. *Robert Redfield and the Development of American Anthropology*. Lanham, MD: Lexington Books.

Wilkinson, Richard, and Kate Pickett. 2010. *The Spirit Level: Why Greater Equality Makes Societies Stronger*. New York: Bloomsbury Press.

Williams, David R. 1998. "Socioeconomic Differentials in Health: A Review and Redirection." *Social Psychology Quarterly* 53:81-99.

Williams, Redford B. 1993. "Lower Socioeconomic Status and Increased Mortality: Early Childhood Roots and the Potential for Successful Interventions." *Journal of the American Medical Association* 279:1745-6.

Wilson, William J., and Richard P. Taub. 2006. *There Goes the Neighborhood*. Chicago: University of Chicago Press.

Wimberly, Dale W. 1990. "Investment Dependence and Alternative Explanations of Third World Mortality: A Cross-National Study." *American Sociological Review* 55:75-91.

Wright, Gavin. 1986. *Old South, New South*. New York: Basic Books.

Wuthnow, Robert. 2012. *Red State Religion*. Princeton, NJ: Princeton University Press.

Young, Frank W. 1967. "Incest Taboos and Social Solidarity." *American Journal of Sociology* 72:589-600.

_____. 1978. "Folktales and Social Structure: A Comparison of Three Analyses of the Star Husband Tale." *Journal of American Folklore* 91:692-699.

——. 1985. "The Informant Survey as a Method for Studying Irrigation Systems." *Journal of Asian and African Studies* XX:56-71.

_____. 1993. "Regional Structure in Sub-Saharan Africa." *Journal of Asian and African Studies* XXVIII:30-41.

____. 1994. "The Goldschmidt Hypothesis in Chile." *Rural Sociology* 59:154-174.

____. 1996. "'Small Town and Mass Society' Revisited." *Rural Sociology* 61:630-648.

____. 2001. "An Explanation of the Persistent Doctor-Mortality Association." *Journal of Epidemiology and Community Health* 55: 80-84.

____. 2001. Putnam's Challenge to Community Sociology. *Rural Sociology* 66:468-474.

——. 2004. "Socioeconomic Status and Health: A Sociological Solution." *Social Theory and Health* 2:124-141.

——. 2006. "Social Problems: A Focus for a New Branch of Public Health?" *Social Theory and Health* 4:264-274.

____. 2009. *The Structural Ecology of Health and Community*. Ithaca, NY: The internet-First University Press. http://dspace.library.-cornell.edu/bitstream/1813/11809/1/Young%20Structural%20Ecology%20Health%20and%20Community.pdf

——. 2012. "Population Health as the Fundamental Criterion of Social Ecology." *Social Indicators Research* 114:229-241.

____. 2013. "What's the Matter with Kansas? A Sociological Answer." *Sociological Forum* 28:864-72

Young, Frank W., and Thomas Lyson. 1993. "Branch Plants and Poverty in the American South." *Sociological Forum* 8:433-50.

Zimmerman, Joseph F. 1995. *State-Local Relations: A Partnership Approach*. New York: Praeger.

Zopf, Paul E. 1992. *Mortality Patterns and Trends in the United States*. Westport, CT: Greenwood.

www.ingramcontent.com/pod-product-compliance
Lightning Source LLC
Chambersburg PA
CBHW021904020426
42334CB00013B/477